Making Sense of Europe

*   *   *   *   *

Making Sense of Europe

*   *   *
*   *   *

Christopher Tugendhat

New York
COLUMBIA UNIVERSITY PRESS
1988

Printed in the United States of America

Library of Congress Cataloging-in-Publication Data

Tugendhat, Christopher, 1937–
  Making Sense of Europe.

  Bibliography: p.
  Includes index.
  1. European Economic Community. I. Title.
HC241.2.T83 1988 337.1'42 87-15871
ISBN 0-231-06682-1 (alk. paper)

Hardback editions of Columbia University Press are Smyth-sewn and printed
on permanent and durable acid-free paper.

To my sons, James and Angus

Contents

Acknowledgements

During my eight years with the European Commission I spoke with many people from many countries about the problems and future of Europe. They have all made a contribution to this book, and I thank them all. However, I owe a special and lasting debt of gratitude to the men and women of different nationalities who worked for me in my cabinet. I will always remember their loyalty, dedication and friendship. Their thoughts and insights have been of incalculable value to me in working out my own ideas. Simon May in particular assisted me in that process. I should also like to thank Paul Lever, who, in addition to all he did for me as a *chef de cabinet*, commented on the final draft of my manuscript, as did John Wyles of the *Financial Times*, whose own writings have themselves done so much to make sense of Europe. None of these individuals is responsible for whatever errors of fact or interpretation may remain. Nor are they in any way bound by my conclusions. But without their help this project could never have been completed. In addition, I thank my agent, Deborah Rogers, and Tony Lacey of Viking for their faith, help and efficiency, and Lavender Hastie for her typing and everything else she has done to facilitate my life since my return to Britain.

ACKNOWLEDGEMENTS

Finally and above all, I thank my wife, Julia, and my sons, James and Angus, for their encouragement, patience and forbearance. Only those who have themselves moved house and decorated a new one, while getting their own professional lives in order, can imagine what it means for a wife to do that while her husband is writing a book to a tight deadline. For all that she has done for me I thank her from the bottom of my heart.

Introduction

From January 1977 until January 1985 I served as a European commissioner; for the first four years as a member of the Commission presided over by Roy Jenkins, and for the second four as a Vice-President under Gaston Thorn. Old hands told me when I arrived in Brussels that I would leave with a deep sense of frustration, and they were right. For much of the time life at the top of the European Community resembles nothing so much as the labours of Sisyphus – endlessly pushing a stone up a hill only to have it crash back to the bottom as soon as it gets within reach of the top. Sisyphus was condemned always to fail. In the Community I found that success came just sufficiently often to encourage one to keep on trying. The rarity provided the incentive, as for an oyster fisherman in search of pearls. Frustration is often accompanied by cynicism and disillusionment, but not in my case. The longer I stayed in Brussels the more convinced I became of the need for the Community, and the more determined that it should be transformed into a Union capable of fulfilling the needs and aspirations of the states and peoples involved. No matter how contentious, detailed or difficult the specific points I was engaged on, I never for a moment doubted that I was part of one of the most important and hopeful political experiments to have been undertaken in this part of the world in modern times.

I was not surprised by either the nature or the extent of the problems I encountered. The countries and people of Western Europe are very different from each other, and have been divided among themselves for centuries. Their sense of nationality and identity is strong. Any attempt to unify them must take these factors into account, and is bound to be accompanied by many set-backs. It will require time to evolve, and will inevitably be complicated and unlike constitutional models devised in other circumstances. These are fundamental points, which are too often forgotten.

My doubts were of a different order. As my experience grew so the conviction took hold that the rhetoric and reality of the Community are out of step with each other, and that both are all too often out of touch with the requirements of the governments and peoples of the member states. I also became increasingly concerned by the extent to which its institutions have made themselves incomprehensible to the public at large. I determined, therefore, to write a book that would explore the reasons for what has happened, explain the motives and objectives of the countries involved and try to establish a basis on which the enterprise might more effectively be carried forward.

Since I began writing at the beginning of 1985 others too have been engaged in trying to set Europe on a new course. With the settlement in 1984 of the dispute over the British budgetary contribution, the most divisive internal issue within the Community in recent years, and the conclusion in 1985 of the enlargement negotiations with Spain and Portugal, the time appeared ripe for new initiatives. National governments and the European Parliament have accordingly been coming forward with new ideas, committees have been reporting and, in September 1985, an inter-governmental conference opened in Luxembourg. Once such a climate of questioning and reconsideration begins it is likely to continue for some time, regardless of the agreements and disagreements recorded in the early stages. The foundations are being laid for the way in which Europe will be organized in the twenty-first century, and this book is my contribution to that process.

My approach owes much to the spirit of one of the Community's great founding fathers, the Belgian statesman Paul Henri Spaak, as exemplified in two quotations. After some years of practical experience in the politics of the 1930s, he warned his rather theoretical colleagues in the Socialist Party that, 'There is a gap between what we say and what we do. That is at the bottom of the trouble. We must do some re-thinking and strike out of our doctrines such elements as events have shown to be untenable.'[1] These words may be applied with equal force to the Europe of today, as may a warning that he issued some years later when the first phase of post-war European co-operation was running into problems. 'The best Europeans,' he said, 'are not those with the most beautiful, generous ideas who become discouraged when they fail to materialize. The good Europeans are those who know where the difficulties lie, who try to solve them, and who never allow themselves to become discouraged.'[2]

* * * 1 * * *
* * *   * * *

Rhetoric and Reality

To attempt a description of the European Community is rather like trying to explain a psychic experience. It exists on so many different planes: the one on which it presents itself; the way in which politicians try to mould it; the actual; and the potential. The overlap between them is often small, and the first two vie with each other in unreality.

Working in Brussels for a prolonged period can itself induce certain dream-like sensations. All the paraphernalia of power and influence on a continental scale is there, or at any rate scattered between Brussels, Luxembourg and Strasbourg. There is a Parliament elected by direct universal suffrage, a Court of Justice, a Council of Ministers to take decisions and the Commission with its responsibilities for initiating proposals and administering policies. Ambassadors from all over the world are accredited to the Community and lobbyists abound. There is a large polyglot press corps for which the Commission arranges daily press conferences and the ambassadors' and lobbyists' numerous on- and off-the-record briefings. There are frequent crises involving breakthroughs and breakdowns, ministerial meetings that go on well into the night and the Parliament threatening thunderbolts against the Commission.

The output of reports, speeches, proposals, trial balloons and leaks from the various institutions is prodigious and appears even greater than it is, as they are often circulated in up to eight languages with a different-coloured title sheet for each. They frequently compete with, and contradict, each other, but they combine to give an impression of importance, excitement and movement to life in the city – Brussels – that the excellent local English-language weekly, *The Bulletin*, used to refer to on its masthead as 'The Capital of Europe'. The words 'Europe' and 'European' are used so often that they come to appear as real and substantial as the modern and impressive buildings from which this tidal wave of paper emanates.

The European economy is described as if it were an entity. Industries are defined in European terms as if their component parts had common interests and were engaged in some gigantic and perpetual struggle against the Americans and Japanese. Political, economic and even social goals are set as if national divisions did not exist, or at least were no greater than those between the different parts of a very large but united political structure. A character in one of Arnold Bennett's plays complains that 'journalists say a thing that they know isn't true in the hope that if they keep on saying it long enough it will be true'.[1] In Brussels and Strasbourg politicians and officials urge them on to do so.

An indication that everything is not as firmly anchored in reality as it seems is provided by the way the protagonists seek to present their views and objectives as 'European' and *communautaire* and to damn those of their opponents as 'anti-European' or anti-*communautaire*. Many insults are hurled by politicians at each other in national capitals, but it is rare for those operating in securely based political systems to accuse their opponents of being less British, French, Dutch or whatever it may be than they themselves.

The real giveaway comes, however, when one buys a newspaper or turns on a television. In Brussels the range of cosmopolitan choice is remarkable. In the newsagents newspapers and magazines from all over Europe jostle for space; the *Irish Times* beside *Il Tempo*; *Le Monde* on top of the Danish *Borsen*; *Die Welt* cheek by jowl with the Spanish *El País*, and so on. In one's living room, thanks to the cable companies, one can tune in to a dozen or more TV channels from six countries. Yet most of the paper spewed out in the Community centres does not find its way into the press or on to the TV screens. The media remain stubbornly convinced that most of the real news is made in their own countries, by the superpowers or in whatever other part of the world happens to be suffering from a disaster at that particular moment. What is more, it is evident that what interests, worries or excites the Irish, Italians, French or Danes on any given day is likely to differ widely. The front pages and headlines are rarely the same. When Europe is covered, it is far more often than not from the point of view of the government of the country concerned or of a national special interest group; hardly ever from an overall European point of view. In short, the Europe that seems so real in Brussels and Strasbourg is like a shadow compared with national governments and national concerns in the member states.

The most telling evidence of that came during the 1984 election campaign for the European Parliament. Nowhere was it a European election in the sense that the electors were primarily, or even secondarily, concerned with what the composition of the European Parliament would be or who would represent them there. Nor were there any great European issues that simultaneously engaged the attention of electors in different countries. It was universally regarded as primarily a national event, fought on national issues and reported in national terms. Indeed the Grand Duchy of Luxembourg made a virtue of this by holding its national election on the same day.

In France it was treated as a sort of qualifying round for the 1986 National Assembly and 1988 Presidential elections in which Lionel Jospin for the Socialists and Madame Simone Veil for the Opposition could show their paces. The most striking personal victory was achieved by the extreme right-wing nationalist Jean-Marie Le Pen, a man whose views would seem to be the very antithesis of any Community ideal. In Belgium, as always at election time, the eternal struggle between Flemish and Walloons played a large part in the proceedings, and the most notable individual victor was Jose Happart, a Francophone mayor in a Flemish province, who achieved national prominence by refusing even to learn the Dutch language spoken by the majority of his compatriots. In Germany and Britain the European election was seen primarily as an opportunity for the still relatively new leaders of the Socialist parties defeated at the previous national elections, Hans-Jochen Vogel and Neil Kinnock, to try out their new teams and images on the national stage.

The absence of a European identity is not only a matter of news and politics. As Jack Lang, France's irrepressible Minister of Culture, has pointed out, 'l'Europe de la Littérature' does not even begin to exist. People simply do not seem interested in reading books written by their neighbours. According to his figures, of 200,000 titles published each year in the Community, translations from one Community country to another account for only 6 to 7 per cent.[2] The market is dominated by the Americans with the British a long way ahead of everyone else, and French literature, to M. Lang's chagrin, attracting all too little attention. It is the same with television. In Brussels during the course of an evening it is sometimes possible to watch *Dallas* five times in three different languages,* but it is unusual to find programmes from one European country being screened in others, with some notable British exceptions.

Why the Rhetoric

As if to bridge the gap between presentation and reality, politicians do not hesitate to put forward proposals that, whatever the small print may say, are designed to give the impression that far-reaching forms of European Union are on the current political agenda and that constitutional innovations can overcome the national and political differences that remain. It is not only 'professional Europeans' pursuing careers in Brussels and Strasbourg who do this.

Chancellor Kohl of the Federal Republic of Germany frequently does so, as for instance in his speech to the Bundestag on 28 March 1984, when he asked, 'Who is prepared to follow us on the way to European political union with the stated objective of a United States of Europe?' Also in 1984, ex-President Valéry Giscard d'Estaing of France put forward a proposal for a President and Vice-President of the European Council – the thrice-yearly gathering of heads of state and government† – to be elected by direct universal suffrage on a Europe-wide basis.[3] Armed with the authority of this mandate, the President would then preside over his fellow heads of state and government and, in a cryptic phrase, 'ensure the external representation of the Union'. In the

---

* Whereas the French- and German-language channels dub the original, the Dutch-language channels use subtitles.
† The phrase 'European Council' is used in Community parlance. In fact the French President is the only head of state who attends.

same year President Mitterrand himself, in a speech to the European Parliament, sought to convey to his audience the impression that in principle he supported its 'Draft Treaty Establishing the European Union', an ambitious and specific plan designed to be implemented over ten years. 'For such an undertaking,' he said, 'France is available. Speaking in her name, I declare her ready to examine and uphold your proposal, which, in its inspiration, suits her.'[4] In each of these cases, men holding or aspiring to the highest offices of state were presenting Europe in a manner that bears no relation to reality and associating themselves with ideas foredoomed to disappointment within any realistic time-scale.

As Abba Eban, the distinguished former Israeli Foreign Minister, has pointed out,[5] those engaged in the affairs of international organizations with high ideals and ambitious aspirations have, ever since the launching of the League of Nations, tended in the context of those organizations to speak in inflated terms quite unlike the language of traditional diplomacy. Hyperbole and exaggeration have always been the hallmark of the League and of its successor the United Nations. Europe is no exception to this rule. From the birth of what might be called the Community system in the early 1950s, and indeed before, the word and the idea have inspired a form of oratory that sometimes becomes almost mystic. It has also frequently been observed that rhetoric tends to be more high flown in national political systems that lack deep roots and are still striving to establish an identity than in those that do not suffer from such disadvantages. The further theory and reality diverge from each other, the greater the apparent need for oratory to fill the gap and to present the world as other than it is. A third factor is the desire to cut a dash on the international stage in order to impress the electors at home. In several countries the best way for a politician to establish his credentials as a statesman and to demonstrate that he possesses a vision that goes beyond his perhaps controversial handling of domestic issues is to put forward far-reaching ideas for the development of Europe. This is not only regarded as 'a good thing'; it has the additional advantage, so long as the ideas are carefully couched, of not offending any domestic special interest group.

It is easy to be cynical about such gesture politics, but it is also necessary to understand the feelings from which they arise. In many parts of Europe the fact that neighbouring countries are living at peace with each other, that frontiers can be crossed easily, that children are not taught at school to hate the next-door country and that the Community exists at all still has a touch of the miraculous about it. No doubt such feelings are stronger in the older generation, as with the retired German banker who told me that having twice crossed the French frontier as part of an invading army he still felt a sense of wonder at being able to do so as a tourist received without rancour. But the folk memory lives on in the younger generation as well and from time to time events occur that bring home the extraordinary contrast between modern Europe and the past. The election of Simone Veil, who as a girl had been taken with other French Jews to a German concentration camp and on whose arm one can still see the tattoo mark of her serial number, as President of the European Parliament, with German and French members dividing for and against her on party rather than national lines, would have been unimaginable in 1945. The occasion was an emotional one for all who witnessed it and thought back to the war years, whether or not they remembered them personally. Too often the British, untouched by so many of the horrors and humiliations of war – 1914–18 as well as 1939–45 – that inspired the Community ideal, still find it hard to comprehend the sentiments that in some countries underlie and underpin it and to which politicians both appeal and respond. It is against this background that the 'Euro-rhetoric' in those countries must be judged.

Rhetoric, accompanied by imaginative proposals and gestures, has a vital role to play in all political systems. It appeals to the emotions and instincts, raises men's and women's eyes from their immediate and parochial concerns to more distant horizons and generates the ground-swell and ultimately the popular demand that are necessary for the attainment of all great objectives. In a multinational system, lacking the cohesion of a nation state, its role is particularly important because of the diversity of views and different attitudes of those who go to make it up. What is being attempted is more difficult and what is being aimed at more distant than in a national system. Rab Butler, in a well-known phrase, described politics as 'the art of the possible'. The role of rhetoric and its accompaniments is to expand the frontiers of the possible and to assist in transforming that which is already contained within them into reality. The style and manner will vary from one language and culture to another.

The French language and tradition, for instance, demand an assertive declaratory form of presentation from leaders and would-be leaders that almost requires to be backed up by dramatic gestures and proposals. Gladstone and Churchill would have understood it well. But now the conditional subjunctive has become almost the characteristic tense of the English language, at any rate in England, and great reliance is placed on metaphor, simile and allusion. Consequently what sounds impressive in French may become pretentious or even self-parody when rendered into English, while what sounds impressive in English can come over as abstract and insipid in French. Roy Jenkins's speeches used to pose great problems for the interpreters in this respect and almost invariably made a more favourable impact on those of his listeners who knew English well than on others. Even greater problems arise between German and English; the German love for broad, often ill-defined, concepts and moral uplift sounds windy and empty to English ears, while English pragmatism strikes the Germans as opportunistic and short-sighted.

Another problem is created by the different meanings that the same words can convey in different languages. In English the words 'European Union' sound clear and firm, like 'United Kingdom' or at least 'United States', and are often taken to convey the same sort of meaning. In other languages and cultures they can imply something less precise and more compatible with separate national identities. In English the concepts of European Union and the continued existence of the nation state seem, *ab initio*, to be incompatible with each other. Elsewhere that is not so. To some, European Union does represent an ambition to replace the nation state, but to most the two are complementary concepts. The nation state and the European Union are seen as enhancing each other, with the latter dependent on the former, extending its scope for effective action and preventing the rivalries inherent in it from running out of control. The same cannot be said of 'United States'. It is impossible to use the words 'United States of Europe' without invoking an image of the United States of America.

Yet it is impossible to regard the United States of America, forged as it was out of thirteen rebellious colonies sharing a common language and culture, as an appropriate model for a group of long-established nation states. Only if national differences and feelings are fully taken into account will it be possible to create a European Union, and even that will be difficult and take a long time. When the impression is given that the

Community is already on the way to becoming a United States of Europe – that heads of state and government are prepared to defer to one of their number following a French-type presidential election on a Europe-wide basis, or that Union of a far-reaching form is an attainable objective of current diplomatic and political activity rather than a long-term goal – public opinion is entitled to expect something dramatic to happen. When the behaviour of governments and relations between them continue much as before, cynicism and disillusion are bound to result. If rhetoric and gestures are to generate political progress they should not be empty or divorced from reality. They should be backed by proposals that are ripe for implementation and that may be seen as steps towards the ultimate objective.

The damage is compounded by those political leaders who give the impression that lack of progress towards unrealistic targets means that Europe is in a state of crisis and perhaps even in danger of falling apart. Leo Tindemans, the Belgian Foreign Minister, provided a typical example of this when he wrote during the European election campaign in April 1984: 'What is at stake is really the idea of Europe ... I still believe in the European Parliament. I see it as a sort of last life-raft of the European ideal.'[6] So did the Parliament's President at that time, the Dutch Socialist, Piet Dankert, with his statement that, 'We must go to the polls because the very survival of the European Community and of our present way of life is at stake.'[7] Confronted by these apocalyptic warnings on the one hand and the statements of Kohl, Giscard d'Estaing and Mitterrand on the other, it is no wonder that public opinion throughout Europe should feel confused about the state of the Community and what is likely to happen to it.

Because it has been in existence for thirty-five years, if the establishment of the European Coal and Steel Community in

1951 is regarded as its date of birth, it is easy to become impatient with the pace of the Community's development and to forget how long political systems need to put down roots. Those who are impatient all too easily underestimate the extremely difficult and delicate nature of the political experiment that it represents.

Enduring Differences

When one looks at the serried ranks of men and women banked up in the hemicycle of the European Parliament, for the most part sitting in multinational party groups rather than in national delegations, with headphones clamped to their ears, there are no obvious national distinctions. Even the headphones, the physical manifestation of their inability to communicate directly with each other, look like a sort of uniform badge of office. It is much the same in the Council of Ministers. The delegation from the country holding the six-monthly rotating presidency sits at one end of a long hollow table with the Commission at the other and the national delegations in alphabetical order along the two sides. Were it not for the signs saying who's who it would be hard to tell them apart. The Italians tend to dress more imaginatively than the Dutch, the Germans look neater than the Irish, and the Danes, the British and the French are more likely to have women in their teams than the others. But there are many exceptions to these rules. It is easy to delude oneself into thinking that, as in Kipling's couplet, 'The colonel's lady an' Judy O'Grady are sisters under their skins.'

Even a few official visits to national capitals ought to be enough to dispel the illusion. As soon as the visitor enters the French Foreign Ministry on the Quai d'Orsay he sees a magnificent portrait of Cardinal Richelieu. Its presence there symbolizes *raison d'état*, the continuity of the French state and the enduring nature of French interests. The grandeur of the major French public buildings and the style and spirit of Paris play their part in moulding the self-confident manner that characterizes French ministers in international negotiations. To emerge from the Trésor in one wing of the Louvre into the Tuileries gardens, with the Carrousel Triumphal arch in the foreground and the Champs-Elysées stretching away to the Arc de Triomphe itself in the distance, is to understand why they invariably seem to feel that, whatever the state of their politics or economy, they must always be at the centre of affairs.

The contrast with Bonn could not be greater. The gimcrack and utilitarian ministry buildings run up in the post-war years retain a temporary and provincial air. Thus, although it is no longer supposed, as was hoped at the beginning, that the occupants will shortly move to Berlin, it is equally hard to believe that the city is the nerve centre of a major European power. The ministries symbolize, and may even help to maintain, the somewhat hesitant and uncertain manner in which the Federal Republic still conducts itself on the international stage, despite its great economic strength.

Europeans may all look pretty much alike and have more in common than divides them – politically, economically, strategically, culturally and in terms of shared moral values. But if an enduring edifice is to be built on the foundations of what binds them together, the degree to which their historical experiences have moulded them in different ways must not be forgotten.

Britain, France, Spain and Portugal have all ruled great overseas empires and retain a variety of links in other parts of the world that are important to their sense of identity. The French and Germans, under many different rulers from Francis I and Charles V, were for hundreds of years locked in an

Table 1 How members of the enlarged EEC compare, 1985

	Population (1,000s)	GDP ($ per capita)	Unemployment (% in 1984)	Consumer price index (1980 = 100)	Employment in (%)		
					Agriculture	Industry	Services
Belgium	9,856	8,126	14.4	134.0	3.0	31.2	65.8
Denmark	5,118	11,020	10.0	139.8	8.5	26.0	65.5
France	54,219	9,538	10.2	149.3	8.1	33.9	58.0
W. Germany	61,638	10,633	8.4	118.4	5.6	42.0	52.4
Greece	9,792	3,505	—	214.5	30.0	28.6	41.4
Ireland	3,483	5,120	16.5	169.2	17.0	29.8	53.2
Italy	56,640	6,208	11.9	174.3	12.4	36.0	51.6
Luxembourg	366	8,721	1.7	136.7	4.7	35.7	59.5
Netherlands	14,313	9,190	14.4	119.6	5.1	27.8	67.1
Portugal	9,997	2,055	10.7	238.4	23.6	35.7	40.7
Spain	37,935	4,237	20.6	163.5	18.0	33.5	48.4
UK	56,341	8,072	11.9	133.4	2.7	33.6	63.7

Sources: EEC and OECD (on the basis of data available in June 1985).

hereditary conflict with results that have helped to mould much of the rest of European history. The modern Federal Republic also continues to carry the burden imposed on it by the Hitler period and all that was done in Germany's name at that time. Holland and Denmark share a deep-seated neutralist tradition. The histories of Ireland, Greece and Luxembourg have been dominated by struggles against predatory and more powerful neighbours, and that of Belgium by the divisions between the two language groups that go to make it up. A central feature of German and Italian history for centuries was the search for the national unity and identity that Britain, France and, above all, Denmark already enjoyed. In some countries, such as France, Germany and Spain, constitutional change has often been accompanied by violence of one sort or another, whereas Britain, Holland, Denmark and Belgium have, for the most part, evolved peacefully. These and many other differences in their historical experience leave their imprint on the way in which European peoples approach contemporary problems in general and what, in Brussels jargon, is called 'the Construction of Europe' in particular.

There are those who argue that in the latter part of the twentieth century Western Europeans, whatever differences of historical experience or contemporary interest they may retain, have no choice but to co-operate. With our continent divided, our empires gone, our economies being overtaken by new and more vigorous rivals and dependent for our defence on the United States in a world riven by rivalries we can barely influence, what choice do we have? What indeed! Benjamin Franklin's famous remark to John Hancock at the signing of the United States Declaration of Independence on 4 July 1776, that 'We must all hang together or, most assuredly, we shall hang separately', can be applied with as much force to contemporary Western

Europe as to the rebellious American colonists to whom it originally referred.

Unfortunately neither history nor people are as straightforward as that. All too often the need does not call forth its own fulfilment. As Richard Mayne has pointed out, 'Few things are less natural for nations than to see their separate problems as facets of a common plight.'[8] The ancient Greeks could not co-operate in the face of the Macedonian threat. When the Turks were advancing into the heart of Europe the Christian kingdoms could not for a long time co-operate against them and even on occasion sought alliances with them. In our own century there was not much unity against a common threat in Europe in the 1930s.

Nor can it be said that economic interdependence necessarily promotes close political relations. In *The Economic Consequences of the Peace*, Keynes describes how, before the outbreak of war in 1914, Germany was the 'central support' round which 'the rest of the European economic system grouped itself and on the prosperity and enterprise of Germany the prosperity of the rest of the Continent mainly depended'.[9] Before August 1914 Germany was Russia's best customer, Britain's second best and France's third best, and these facts did nothing whatsoever to inhibit the formation of antagonistic alliances nor to prevent the war.

Experience shows that different races, language groups and religious communities find it extremely hard to share a confined space and to contend with common problems, which is the predicament the member states of the Community, huddled together on the western tip of the Eurasian land-mass, find themselves in. This is true of cities and it is true of countries, as the histories of Lebanon, Cyprus, Ireland and Belgium, in their different ways, all show. Switzerland, where people who speak different languages and subscribe to different branches of the Christian religion run a successful Confederation free from inter-communal strife, provides a rare example to the contrary. The Swiss achievement is considerable, but it is worth remembering that more than 500 years elapsed from the first three cantons coming together in an 'Everlasting League' in 1291 and the last, Geneva, joining the Confederation in 1848. During that time and since, habits of co-operation and the difficult concept of shared and divided loyalties were able to take root gradually.

It is against this background that the Community's record since 1951 must be judged. It is far removed from the federalist aspirations of some of its founders, bears little relation to much of the rhetoric that surrounds it and is quite unripe for the sort of constitutional innovations sometimes suggested for it. Yet in the light of Europe's past and the difficulties any such enterprise must face, it has achieved a great deal and, notwithstanding its omissions and failures, it has the scope to do much more. After all, the paraphernalia of power and influence on a continental scale would not be present in Brussels, Luxembourg and Stras-bourg if there was no substance below the surface froth in those centres. The ambassadors from all over the world would not be appointed, the lobbyists would not be able to justify their fees and the ministers would not spend so many hours negotiating in the Council of Ministers unless real interests were at stake. To quote Abba Eban again, 'Europe may be lagging behind its own vision, but it is still ahead of everyone else in the quest for an identity transcending the sovereignty of separate states.'[10]

In the Beginning

To measure the nature and extent of that achievement it is necessary to go back to the beginning. There is no better place at which to start than the Declaration of 9 May 1950 with which Robert Schuman, the then French Foreign Minister, launched the proposal for a European Coal and Steel Community. Its initial paragraphs are as follows:

World peace cannot be safeguarded without the making of constructive efforts proportionate to the dangers which threaten it. The contribution which an organized and living Europe can bring to civilization is indispensable to the maintenance of peaceful relations. In taking upon herself for more than twenty years the role of champion of a united Europe, France has always had as her essential aim the service of peace. A united Europe was not achieved; and we had war. Europe will not be made all at once or according to a single general plan. It will be built through concrete achievements, which first create a *de facto* solidarity. The gathering together of the nations of Europe requires the elimination of the age-old opposition of France and Germany. The first concern in any action undertaken must be these two countries.

With this aim in view, the French government proposes to take action immediately on one limited but decisive point. The French government proposes to place Franco-German production of coal and steel under a common higher authority, within the framework of an organization open to the participation of the other countries of Europe. The pooling of coal and steel production will immediately provide for the setting up of common bases for economic development as a first step in the federation of Europe, and will change the destinies of those regions which have long been devoted to the manufacture of munitions of war, of which they have been the most constant victims.

It is hard to conceive of a more imaginative or daring approach. After the Franco-Prussian War of 1870–71 and the Great War of 1914–18, first the new German Empire and then France sought to drive home its victory to the maximum possible extent. Although France after 1945 was in the victors' camp only by courtesy of the United States and Britain and in a weaker diplomatic position than after 1918, there were many in France who would have liked to have pursued the same policy as Clemenceau at Versailles if only they could. They were fearful of the consequences of Germany's rehabilitation and some were still anxious to annex the Saar. For a French government in those circumstances to suggest that France and Germany should be partners in a common enterprise took great courage. The reasons for taking the initiative are discussed in the next chapter. Now is the time to consider the Declaration itself, the sequence of events and their consequences.

The central points of the Declaration and of the thinking behind it are clear. In the first place it is based on the belief, derived from history, that the peace of Europe depends on Franco-German reconciliation. From this it is but a short step to the second point, which is that their reconciliation must be the rock on which future developments will be based. Although the prospect of a European federation is held out, the third point is that it is concrete achievements not general plans which matter, which is why the specific proposal relating to coal and steel manufacture is put forward. Finally while others are invited to join they are left in no doubt that the proponents of the plan intend to go ahead anyway; others are welcome, but not indispensable. In London a few days after making his Declaration, Schuman was asked, 'How many countries are needed to make the plan work?' 'If necessary,' he replied, 'we shall go ahead with only two.'[11] It is essential to grasp these points in order to make sense of all that has happened since.

Everything was prepared in great secrecy, but before putting his proposals to the French cabinet Schuman informed the US Secretary of State, Dean Acheson, of his intentions and made sure that they would be accepted in Bonn by sending a secret emissary to Chancellor Konrad Adenauer. The British government heard about the Schuman proposals only after the French cabinet had agreed to allow them to go ahead.

When the French ambassador, René Massigli, called on the Foreign Secretary, Ernest Bevin, to deliver the message, Bevin, with the instinctive grasp for which he remains famous, replied, 'I think something has changed between our two countries.'[12] Acheson in his memoirs recalls Bevin's rage at being excluded from the circle of consultation and the suspicions it aroused. His reminder to the British that they had been in touch with Washington but not Paris before the previous year's devaluation of sterling did nothing to calm the situation. He also records the judgement that, 'Despite my most earnest arguments, in the next few days Britain made her great mistake of the post-war period by refusing to join in negotiating the Schuman Plan.'[13]

Even without this inauspicious start it is barely conceivable that Britain would have taken up Schuman's invitation to participate in the negotiations. It was entirely out of keeping with the British mood at that time. To Monnet, as to many others on the Continent, Britain with its unique post-war prestige was 'the one great power in Europe' that could provide 'a nucleus around which a European Community might be formed'.[14] But in the years between 1945 and 1950 the British had repeatedly shown in relation to the negotiations surrounding the establishment of the Council of Europe and its early operations, as well as on other matters, that they did not share the aspirations taking root on the Continent. As Monnet's friend and former wartime colleague Lord Plowden put it, when recalling the ideas Monnet had floated in London in the late 1940s and the way they had been received, 'We'd won the war and we weren't ready to form any special links with the continent'[15] – a comment that sums up the attitude not just of the British establishment in those years but of the British people in general.

Monnet himself recognized this and in some notes he made in the summer of 1950 wrote:

Britain has no confidence that France and the other countries of Europe have the ability or even the will effectively to resist a possible Russian invasion . . . Britain believes that in this conflict continental Europe will be occupied but that she herself, with America, will be able to resist and finally conquer. She therefore does not wish to let her domestic life or the development of her resources be influenced by any views other than her own, and certainly not by continental views.[16]

The Labour Party in a pamphlet published in June of that year gave another reason for not joining: 'In every respect except distance we in Britain are closer to our kinsmen in Australia and New Zealand on the far side of the world than we are to Europe. We are closer in language and in origins, in social habits and institutions, in political outlook and economic interest.'[17] The pamphlet was prepared by the party's international committee whose chairman was the leader of the Labour delegation to the Council of Europe and former Chancellor of the Exchequer, Hugh Dalton, and approved by Prime Minister Clement Attlee as well as by Bevin, which gave it considerable authority. The committee's secretary, who prepared the draft, was Denis Healey.[18]

So Britain remained out. Her doubts about both the capacity of the continentals and the wisdom of co-operating with them were so strong that she also decided against participating in the negotiations that led in 1957 to the formation of the European Economic Community and the now nearly forgotten Euratom,* despite the strong desire of Holland, Belgium, Luxembourg and

---

* The European Coal and Steel Community, the European Economic Community and Euratom were merged in 1967. As a result, the word 'Communities' rather than 'Community' is sometimes used and is technically more correct.

Italy, which had all accepted Schuman's original invitation and joined the ECSC, to have her aboard. With these countries involved, however, the Franco-German enterprise became, from the outset, a European one and the European became Franco-German. This has proved to be of the utmost importance.

The European Coal and Steel Community created a comprehensive system for regulating its members' coal and steel industries, the foundations on which their industrial economies were at that time based and the cause of many past rivalries that had helped to bring about war. It was seen, as Gaston Thorn has succinctly put it, as 'an attempt to institutionalize the riches that had caused earlier conflicts so that in future they would promote co-operation'. The Treaty of Rome, which established the European Economic Community, took that co-operation a major step forward with its commitment to the creation of a Common Market and a Common Agricultural Policy.

That package was of immense significance and provided the basis on which the whole Community edifice was subsequently constructed. It gave the Federal Republic of Germany, cut off from its traditional markets in the East, continental-scale opportunities for its manufactured goods and France similar opportunities for its agriculture. Both countries were guaranteed protection against competition from the produce of the rest of the world by the introduction of the principle of 'Community Preference'. In the case of industrial goods the level of protection reflected the needs of the less efficient industries in the Community, many of which were in France, while in agriculture it was designed to safeguard the least efficient farmers so that when common prices were established their base point was the high German cereal price on which the prosperity of German agriculture had long been built. A balanced and symmetrical trade-off was thereby established which satisfied the basic economic interests of the two countries and enabled each to gain from the relative inefficiencies of the other. As the German refusal in 1985 to contemplate a significant reduction in cereal prices demonstrated, the consequences of this trade-off are still very much with us.

The deal suited the economic interests and aspirations of the other four but, as will become apparent in the next chapter, their reasons for becoming involved were never primarily economic. Political and idealistic motives both played an important part. There was, however, one other factor which was also of great significance.

As the histories of Italy and the Benelux countries – Belgium, Holland and Luxembourg – show, it is the fate of small and relatively weak countries to be trampled on when their larger neighbours make war and to have their interests squeezed when those neighbours make up. From the point of view of those four the beauty of the Schuman and subsequent proposals was that they held out the prospect of guarantees of equality with the larger powers undreamt of in previous attempts at European co-operation. In the age of Metternich and the Concert of Europe, smaller powers were pawns in a great game. In the Community a system of rules, obligations and procedures of a detailed kind was laid down and has since been further developed to guarantee that the rights of all members will be respected and that reconciliation between the larger ones will not be at the expense of the smaller. This is a major reason why the Community has proved so enduring and why it, rather than any other model, came to be so widely regarded, in the words of the former German Chancellor Helmut Schmidt, as 'the core of that part of Europe in which we live and which provides the political chance to shape the future of our societies'.[19]

An Assessment

In terms of most of the principal points laid down in Schuman's Declaration of 9 May 1950 Europe has done well in the thirty-five years that have followed. Franco-German reconciliation has been achieved to the extent that the Paris–Bonn axis is regarded both as a fixed point in the European firmament and as the central one in everybody else's calculations. The Community that has been built around it has also become the framework within which most of the countries of Western Europe conduct their relations, try to reconcile their differences and seek to co-operate in response to internal and external challenges. First Britain accompanied by Ireland and Denmark joined, then Greece, and finally Spain and Portugal. As soon as the last three had thrown off their dictatorships and returned to democracy it seemed natural that they should apply for membership, which is a tribute not just to the economic benefits they hope to acquire, but also to the Community's political inspiration. In historical terms a great ingathering of European people has been achieved, and it is necessary only to consider the histories of Germany, Italy and Switzerland to appreciate that by the standards of the past it has not taken long.

It is no wonder that it should have been accompanied by problems. For a quarter of a century, since the initial British application in August 1961, the Community has been either preparing for enlargement negotiations, engaged in them or adjusting to their consequences, and for the last decade or so in all three at once. The disruption has been considerable as countries with very different histories and traditions from the original six have had to be incorporated. Nor is it surprising that many of the problems should have centred on Britain. It was only to be expected that such an important country would have greater difficulty in adjusting to a system created around two other large powers than would most smaller states. Three is always a difficult number, in inter-state relations just as much as in those between individuals, especially when one is a latecomer.

Despite these achievements the Community is not perceived as a success by most people in Europe. The rhetoric referred to earlier is partly to blame since it has created unrealistic expectations and also drawn attention away from the fact that apart from anything else the Community is a political system with all that this implies. By definition the process of striking a balance between rival and conflicting interests, reconciling differences and formulating policies is a noisy and disputatious one. As the United States shows, the larger the area contained within a single political system and the more diverse the geographical and other interests involved, the noisier and more protracted it becomes. So does Canada which also demonstrates how linguistic and cultural differences can intensify political disagreements to the point where an edifice with 100 years or so of history behind it may tremble. It is not surprising, therefore, that the Community's walls should shudder from time to time.

Another reason for public disenchantment is, however, more substantial. The expansion of the Community's membership and the creation of a European political system have not been matched by results. In particular the ideas of the early days designed to lead the way towards a federal Europe have turned out disappointingly. Recent experiments of a more pragmatic nature have, up to a point, made up for this, but taken as a whole the array of concrete achievements has not lived up to expectations, though it is more impressive than is sometimes supposed.

The Internal Record

At the heart of the Community lies the Internal Market, an interconnecting set of trading links that combine to create such a web of interdependence between the member states as to provide the basis on which a single economic system could be created. The basic statistics are set out in Tables 1 and 2. The percentages may vary somewhat from one year to another depending on exchange rate fluctuations and the extent to which one economy or another is sucking in imports or clamping down on demand. For instance, the high level of the dollar in 1983 and 1984 led to increased opportunity for all European exporters in the United States and made American exports less competitive in Europe. These variations apart, a clear picture emerges. For all the older member states the rest of the Community is not just their principal export market and source of imports, but overwhelmingly so. In other words, jobs and opportunities in these states are dependent to a considerable degree on decisions taken in other Community capitals, and thus each government has a strong interest in being able to influence those of its partners. It has not been possible to gather figures on the same basis for Spain and Portugal. But even before entering the Community their trade was deeply bound up with it. In 1983 nearly half Spain's exports and more than half of Portugal's were to their future partners. What is true of the older members thus applies with equal force to them.

The fact of that interdependence is not new. Keynes's description of pre-1914 Germany as the central support around which the other European economies grouped themselves bears a striking resemblance to the contemporary scene. The structure of European industry may have changed out of all recognition since then and not many of the companies that were prominent

Table 2 Basic trade statistics: imports/exports, calendar year 1984

%	BL./LX.	Denmark	France	W. Germany	Greece	Ireland	Italy	Netherlands	UK
Imports from other member states	66.7	46.4	50.3	48.2	47.0	64.7	43.3	53.1	44.7
Imports from Japan	2.2	3.9	2.6	4.2	7.6	3.4	1.6	2.3	4.8
Imports from the USA	6.0	5.2	7.7	7.1	2.9	16.5	6.1	8.9	12.0
Imports from the rest of the world	25.1	44.5	39.4	40.5	42.5	15.4	49.0	35.7	38.5
Exports to other member states	69.3	43.6	48.9	47.8	54.1	68.6	45.4	71.9	44.8
Exports to Japan	0.8	2.8	1.1	1.4	1.1	1.7	1.1	0.6	1.3
Exports to the USA	6.0	9.8	8.1	9.6	8.3	9.7	10.9	5.0	14.5
Exports to the rest of the world	23.9	43.8	41.9	41.2	36.5	20.0	42.6	22.5	39.4

in those days have survived to hold leading positions today. But given a period of prolonged peace Germany invariably appears to play the leading economic role in Europe, providing the basis for the prosperity of others, and in turn depending on them for its own.

What is new, however, is the way in which the European market is run. In the period before 1914 and between the wars each national market was surrounded by tariff walls. In modern Europe there are no tariffs and a plant can be built in one Community country in the certainty that its output will circulate freely throughout the rest without any danger of such barriers being imposed. There are also Community rules that provide guarantees of access that can be upheld in the European Court when attempts are made to restrict them. Such attempts frequently are made, but as the outcome of such celebrated cases as British lamb in France and French UHT milk in Britain show, the law eventually wins through. In earlier times no such redress existed. A framework of rules has also been established to ensure that the terms and conditions on which goods are sold in different markets should be brought into line and subjected to decisions taken on the basis of Community procedures. Finally, there is a set of competition rules designed to prevent individual governments providing subsidies that would give their companies unfair advantages over those of their partners and to prevent the abuse of corporate power. It is thanks to these rules that the individual member states have been restrained from bidding against each other to attract new investment and to boost their own companies in a manner that would have cost them far more than any short-term benefits they might have obtained.

None the less, compared with the United States, the Community still has a long way to go before it can claim to be a real common market. The continued existence of complicated frontier controls, differing technical and other standards and a host of other non-tariff barriers to trade bear witness to that. A lorry driver carrying goods from, say, Britain to Italy requires a mass of forms to enable him to cross the various frontiers involved. He can be subjected to delays at any one of them, and sometimes to deliberate obstruction. It has been estimated that the cost of frontier formalities alone is of the order of 5 to 10 per cent of the pre-tax value of the traded goods, and that the time consumed as a result of such delays represents a loss of about £500 million a year. In the case of services, such as offering insurance contracts across frontiers, the situation is far worse than with goods, since many of the original obstacles to free trade still remain. At times in Brussels one has the impression that as soon as one set of barriers and restraints has been removed the next is even worse, and that when that has been dealt with others have somehow been constructed to take its place.

The biggest offenders of all are governments in the area over which they have the most direct control, namely public procurement, which accounts for between 7 and 10 per cent of total Community gross domestic product. In 1982 virtually 100 per cent of central government supply spending in Italy went to Italian companies; the figure for France was 99.91 per cent, for Germany 99.7 per cent and for Britain 98.3 per cent; Holland, Belgium and Denmark were all at 96.6 per cent or more.[20] These figures exaggerate the degree of national preference because some national suppliers are subsidiaries of foreign companies, but the general picture is clear enough. The gap between what governments say they want to achieve in Europe and what they actually do is very wide.

Notwithstanding these faults, too much pessimism would be out of place. It took black people in the United States many decades to secure their full civil rights, but those rights were inherent in the constitution if only they could be dragged out and applied. The same is true of the free movement of goods and services and free competition within the European Community. What creates so much disillusion, as it did for the black minority in the United States, is the length of time and the bitter wrangling required, to which in the European case must be added the fact that progress in recent years has been so much slower than it was earlier.

Vested interests fight every inch of the way to protect their own positions. These include companies wanting to defend markets against foreign competition and bureaucracies afraid that their own *raison d'être* will be threatened if restrictions are abolished. In most countries the customs service is particularly guilty in this respect and can often rely on governments not to attack its privileges. I remember once putting the case for a change that would speed the passage of goods through French frontier controls to a notably Community-minded Finance Minister in Paris, who told me that he simply could not face the political difficulties involved in a row with such an entrenched element in the national bureaucracy at a time when he had other more pressing problems to deal with. Governments also take a view on where their overall balance of interest lies. If they think their national companies will benefit from freer competition they support it, as with the British government and insurance. If they think their own firms will lose out they will probably fight a prolonged rearguard action against it, as the German government has done in the same case.

Yet despite these and other shortcomings, future historians will probably record that the way in which the achievements of the early years were maintained and markets kept open during the successive oil shocks and the deep economic recession of the

1970s and early 1980s in itself constitutes a considerable success. By comparison with the 1930s it certainly does. But that is a negative success. To contemporaries it is the loss of momentum and the actual reality that matter, not the reasons why.

If the trouble with the Common Market is that it has not been brought to fruition, the same cannot be said of its *alter ego*, the Common Agricultural Policy, universally known as the CAP. The CAP is beyond doubt a fully developed Community policy. The vast bulk of what the land produces – milk, meat, cereals, olive oil, wine, hops, fruit and vegetables (though not potatoes), cotton, tobacco and much else besides – is subject to Community 'regimes'. The major decisions affecting their price and production are taken in Brussels by the Council of Ministers on the basis of proposals from the Commission. The trouble lies with the way the procedure has worked out in practice. It provides a case study of how difficult it is for the political bargaining process, involving ministers from a large number of different countries, to set priorities and allocate scarce resources.

The central problem is that although the policy is common in the sense that it applies to the whole Community each national minister is above all interested in what he can secure for his own country. By comparison with that imperative they care little for the overall balance of the policy, or what it costs. For many years the Commission has been putting forward proposals designed to curb costs and limit excess production. They can be criticized for not being sufficiently ambitious on some occasions, but they have invariably pointed in that direction. Ministers from northern countries have responded by welcoming the proposals in relation to Mediterranean products while arguing for those concerning northern products to be softened or even abandoned. The Mediterranean ministers have taken the opposite view.

Many days and nights have then been devoted to detailed negotiations at the end of which both sides have generally agreed on a compromise giving each part of what it wants so that all, or nearly all, ministers can claim a negotiating triumph when they return home to their national parliaments. In most years the European Parliament has, meanwhile, been passing resolutions in favour of higher spending all round.

Within the northern and Mediterranean groups individual ministers argue for their own interests, but alliances between producers of the same commodity are also formed and ministers influence each other. If the Greeks, say, adopt a specially tough line on olive oil and this is known outside, as it generally would be, that both stiffens the other olive oil producers and makes it harder for them to compromise. With the arrival of Spain and Portugal the Mediterranean lobby, which has tended to be rather outgunned by the northerners in recent years, receives notable reinforcement, and the pivotal role of France as a producer of both northern and Mediterranean products will become even more crucial than before.

The result of the way in which the Agriculture Council works has been escalating costs and surplus production on a massive scale. Between 1979 and 1984 expenditure rose by 76 per cent, and by the outset of the latter year the Community's excess of production over consumption was 15 per cent for cereals, 19 per cent for sugar, 27 per cent for dairy products and 27 per cent for wine. In order to dispose of some of these surpluses on world markets, vast export subsidies have had to be paid and in early 1985 they were estimated to be running at an annual rate of £5 billion, or about 34 per cent of total agricultural spending through the Community budget.

The extravagances of the CAP, the surpluses it generates and the measures taken to dispose of them have helped to sour public attitudes towards the Community in all parts of Europe. But because of the policy's central position in the basic compromise on which the Community is based, because of the difficulties inherent in getting ten countries to agree on a matter of fundamental concern to all and the strength of the political and economic interests that benefit from it, reform has proved extremely difficult. Another reason paradoxically has been the Community's failure to develop a comprehensive range of spending policies in other fields. Because of that it has often been argued that 'the CAP is the only policy we have and must not be endangered', as if that was a reason for not tackling its underlying problems. As long ago as 1977 I made a proposal designed to ensure that Agriculture Ministers would have to take their decisions within a framework previously established in agreement with Finance Ministers, which would take into account wider economic and financial considerations. It received little support from my Commission colleagues or in national capitals, and not until 1984 when the Community was at the limit of its financial 'own resources' was a system of 'budgetary discipline' put into effect.

Some heads of government must bear a large measure of responsibility both for the CAP's failings and for the public disillusionment to which they have given rise. They have so often spoken of the need for change while letting their Agricultural Ministers carry on as before. As German Chancellor, Helmut Schmidt was second to none in his critiques of what had gone wrong, but it was his Agriculture Minister, the formidable barrel-shaped Bavarian Josef Ertl, who did more than most to push up costs and to generate surpluses. A similar and even more striking dichotomy exists between the present German government's calls for financial stringency in the Community's budget during 1984 and the action of its Agriculture Minister, Ignaz Keichle, another powerful and rotund Bavarian, in invoking 'a vital national interest' to prevent a cut in cereal prices in 1985 – at a time when the German government was arguing that the national veto should be abolished.

The German dilemma can be simply stated and shows how hard it is for governments to be consistent when arguing for the better management of Community policies while seeking to defend the national interest. On the one hand Bonn disapproves of agricultural surpluses and of the cost and the trade disputes with the United States and other countries involved in disposing of them. On the other its own farmers are among the principal beneficiaries of the high cereal prices from which so many other excessive prices derive and which are thus a root cause of those surpluses, costs and trade disputes. When faced with a Commission proposal to reduce cereal prices or even just to set them at more realistic levels, the German government must balance the sectional interests of its farmers against the broader needs of the CAP; there is no doubt which can bring the more painful pressure to bear. This dilemma is particularly acute for Germany and other countries in agriculture because of the nature of the CAP, but it is one that exists to some degree in most policy areas, especially those involving expenditure.

It used to be thought that the CAP would prove to be the first of a balanced array of Community spending policies. A social fund to help the member states with training and re-training schemes and a regional development fund to help them develop their poorer and more isolated regions were set up. It was hoped these would form the basis on which employment and regional policies – organized, like the CAP, on a Community-wide basis – would be established. The outlines of impressive plans for industry, energy, research and transport were sketched out. But all have remained minute by comparison with what is done at the national level. If agriculture is extracted from the Community budget, what is left for other policies amounts to the equivalent of only about 1.2 per cent of the total spending of national governments. The hope that common policies commonly financed would one day form the arches that would link together the various national economies and make possible the long and difficult process of fitting national economies together into a coherent and mutually compatible whole has had to be abandoned.

Table 3   Community budget, 1984

	ECUs (million)	%
Agricultural guarantee	18,333	67.3
Agricultural guidance	675	2.5
Regional policy	1,455	5.3
Social expenditure	1,394	5.1
Energy, research, industry	719	2.6
Co-operation and development	897	3.3
Fishing	112	0.4
Transport	34	0.1
Education and culture	19	0.1
Environment and consumers	16	0.1
Administration	1,237	4.5
Reimbursements (mainly of member states)	1,150	4.3
Reserve	1,207	4.4

Note: The figures are for payment appropriations rather than commitment appropriations. They do not include the figures for the European Coal and Steel Community nor for the European Development Fund, which are entirely separate.

Source: European Commission.

There are several reasons for this. One is the changing attitude towards public expenditure. When the original plans were conceived it was on a steadily rising trend in the member states and enjoyed a wide measure of public support. High spending at the Community level seemed to be its natural concomitant. The change in attitudes on this point in the member states has naturally reduced their willingness to fund Community programmes. But that is not the only factor, nor even the most important. It was also thought in the early days that the richer countries would be prepared to make substantial transfers of wealth to the poorer. For reasons that will be described in the next chapter that theory was invalidated by the early 1970s, if not before. The richer states proved not only unwilling to make such transfers, but also determined that at least some part of every fund should be spent on their territory as well as in the poorer states. It thus became impossible for the Community to devise a coherent theory of what objectives should be pursued by the regional and social funds on a European basis regardless of frontiers and to concentrate expenditure accordingly.

In the light of such considerations and against the background of the conduct of the CAP, the member states have not surprisingly proved unable to reach agreement on substantial industrial, technological or research programmes to be financed through the Community budget. There are a few bright spots, such as the Esprit programme designed to encourage pre-competitive research in the field of information technology, which was launched with a great fanfare in 1984. But its budget of about £950 million – half from the Community and half from the private sector over five years – is modest by international industrial standards.

Despite the modest scale of most of its activities, the rise of agricultural expenditure during the late 1970s and early 1980s was so great that in 1984 the Community found itself at the limit of its financial 'own resources'. Faced with the choice of substantially increasing them in order to revive the original dream or agreeing to only a modest increase, the European Council decided on the latter, although because of the complexities of the system many did not realize this at the time.

The Community's financial arrangements are unique.[21] Whereas other international organizations are funded by contributions from member state governments paid according to a pre-arranged key, the Community's resources belong to it as of right. They consist of customs duties and import levies on agricultural produce, which are paid over to Brussels from wherever they are collected, and a percentage of the Value Added Tax charged in the member states. When the scale of the CAP and other spending policies for the following year has been decided in the annual budget procedure the Commission adds up the likely revenue from the customs duties and levies, calculates how much will be needed from the VAT to bridge the gap and says what the amount should be – 0.9 per cent, 1.3 per cent, etc.* Initially the upper limit was fixed at 1 per cent but at Fontainebleau in 1984 the heads of state and government agreed to ask their national parliaments to increase that to 1.4 per cent.

This was less generous than it appears at first sight because the yield from the other two sources is declining in real terms. Moreover the cost of disposing of agricultural surpluses is certain to remain high for many years to come; there will be bills to pay arising out of the admission of Spain and Portugal, and the rebate on the British contribution, also agreed at Fontainebleau, has to be provided. The amount of money available to increase other spending programmes will thus be modest by most national standards. If they are to have any significant impact on

---

* The assessment that gives rise to the actual transfers is made on a harmonized basis. This overcomes the anomalies that would otherwise arise from the different rates and coverage of the tax in the different countries.

the places where they are most needed, their objectives will have to be much more selective than in the past. It is also likely that a growing number of activities carried out under Community auspices will be financed on an individual basis outside the budget. This will be anathema to the European Parliament, whose principal powers relate to the budget, but is already the case for the European Development Fund though which the major part of the Community's assistance to developing countries is provided.

In other fields of activity not involving common expenditure programmes, the record is rather better. Steel, one of the centre-pieces of Schuman's original plan, is a case in point. When the member states found the overcapacity crisis in that industry running out of control, the 'Manifest Crisis' provisions of the Treaty of Paris were invoked in October 1980, so that each nation would not try to save its own firms and plants at the expense of the rest. A special Community regime, with the Commission playing the central role, was established for determining production quotas, prices, the rate of run-down and subsidies, and for negotiating voluntary restraint agreements with the principal outside suppliers. In 1982 an arrangement to safeguard the Community's exports to the United States on the basis of agreed limits was added. In the summer of 1984 Viscount Etienne Davignon, the commissioner who then had the main responsibility in this field, was able to claim on the Commission's behalf:

Had we not taken action the common market in steel would have ceased to function because each country would have protected itself from its neighbour. We would not have secured an agreement from the United States. Governments would not have been convinced of the need for restructuring which was only feasible at European level. And the war between producers would have made the process even more painful. Prices would have fallen by 25 to 30 per cent – and even more money would have had to be found to rescue steel firms. Today a slimmed-down European steel industry is in sight.[22]

The way in which the steel crisis regime was organized and the Commission executed its responsibilities was widely attacked. Steel workers showed they understood where the key decisions were being taken by organizing demonstrations to the Council of Ministers and Commission buildings in Brussels, along streets and avenues previously followed by the farmers. In Germany, which tended to feel that its more efficient industry was being asked to make undue sacrifices on behalf of others that could not or would not put their own houses in order, the criticisms were particularly strong. With so many jobs at stake and so many regions dependent on the steel industry, such attacks were inevitable. But whenever the member states had to decide whether to continue with the Community-wide crisis measures or to take back more of the responsibility themselves, not one was ever prepared to risk the latter course.

Another example of an industry in trouble being helped to adjust on a Community-wide basis is textiles. In this case the common external trade policy was the main weapon used by the Commission to negotiate first the Multifibre Arrangement and then a series of bilateral agreements with its leading low-wage suppliers. To back this up measures were taken to keep state aid in check, a Community programme to support research was proposed, and payments were made from the regional and social funds. It cannot be said that the industry's performance has since justified the help it received, and after a prolonged period of special assistance there is now a case to be made for a more liberal regime. But as an example of member states working together on a common basis, the Multifibre Arrangement and its consequential programme remain impressive.

Steel and textiles are problem industries involving a large number of member states where the arguments in favour of joint action were so strong as to be self-evident. In other sectors of industry, as was pointed out above, the Community's involvement is small. Outside the formal framework of the Community, however, and in the context of a less structured form of European co-operation there have been some notable achievements. Three that stand out are the Tornado military aircraft, the Airbus and the Ariane rocket project. Separate companies with different memberships produce the Tornado and Airbus, but taken together they have enabled the aircraft industries of Britain, France, Germany, Italy and Spain to compete with the Americans, while Ariane has enabled European technology to hold its own with the Americans and Russians in putting satellites into space.

There are some important lessons to be drawn from these examples which are relevant to much else in a European context. The first is that the most effective spur to common action is a common challenge commonly perceived. In steel it was the world-wide overcapacity crisis, coupled with the fear that the common market in the commodity would break down while Europe would be swamped by imports and shut out of the American market. With the Tornado, Airbus and Ariane it was the awareness that unless Europeans could find a way to work together the Americans would scoop the pool.

The second lesson is that to be effective any common undertaking must begin with a set of limited, explicit and mutually compatible objectives. That is not the case with the CAP and the other spending programmes, and the clash of national interests makes it very difficult to introduce them later on. The problems of co-operation are such that unless those delegated to run an operation, whether it is the Commission or another agency, have a clear mandate they are likely to prove insuperable.

The third lesson is that ideally only those countries with interests directly at stake should be involved. In some cases as with the Airbus this will mean a small number of participants. In others, such as steel, agriculture or, for instance, the current attempts to create a Community-wide market in telecommunications, all can be essential. On occasion it is also sensible not to think in exclusively Community terms. Ariane, for example, includes seven Community countries – France, Germany, Britain, Belgium, Holland, Denmark and Spain – and two non-members, Sweden and Switzerland.

A collection of eclectic enterprises along these lines lacks the intellectual completeness and inspirational quality of the earlier concept of a set of common policies commonly financed acting as arches to link the economies of the member states together. Even so, they represent concrete achievements, and the idea of moulding national economies together in a compatible whole has not been abandoned. It lives on in a different form through the European Monetary System (EMS), established in December 1978* on the basis of an idea put forward by Roy Jenkins as President of the Commission and taken up in a modified form by Chancellor Helmut Schmidt and President Giscard d'Estaing.[23] It has proved to be a most powerful form of economic policy co-ordination, and in the ECU has spawned a remarkable new form of international money that by 1983 had become third only to the dollar and the Deutschmark in terms of international bond issues.†

---

* It actually began operations in March 1979.
† In English ECU stands for European Currency Unit. In French it is the name of a famous medieval coin.

The EMS too demonstrates the adaptability of the European idea and the capacity of those wishing to pursue it to adjust to the circumstances in which they find themselves. Ideally all nine countries that were members of the Community when it was launched should have become full members. But faced with the fact that the British were not prepared to enter the exchange rate mechanism that constitutes the heart of the arrangement, the principal protagonists of the plan had to decide whether or not to proceed without them. They did so without any form of treaty on the basis of a gentlemen's agreement.

Events have justified them. It is always dangerous to claim too much on behalf of monetary systems since this is a field in which success and failure can follow each other with bewildering rapidity, and the chain of cause and effect is open to different interpretations. The first six years of the EMS and its exchange rate mechanism have, however, proved a remarkable success both in terms of reducing the variability of exchange rates and in encouraging co-operation between the participants. It owes much to two innovations compared with the Bretton Woods system that have proved to be of great importance. Firstly, currency realignment decisions are taken collectively. The member states do not simply take a note of a parity change by an individual country, they negotiate a mutually acceptable set of new parities with strong currency countries revaluing at the same time as the weaker ones devalue. Secondly, the realignment decisions are taken on the basis of a collective assessment of the economic measures judged necessary to support the parity changes in both the strong and weak currency countries. As a result the EMS has proved to be both more effective and more symmetrical than the earlier world-wide system.

This in turn promotes continuous frank and detailed exchanges between the participants, which have enabled them to make equally continuous slight adjustments to their policies in the light of both their own domestic needs and what is happening in the other economies. The process is rather like a convoy of ships at sea each reacting independently to the winds and tides while seeking to do so in a manner that keeps it in formation with the rest. This is a far cry from the old ideas of rules enforced by central institutions. But as Raymond Barre, the former French Prime Minister and Vice-President of the Commission, has pointed out, 'International institutions are in the end severely limited by national sovereignty'.[24] A flexible system is more likely to bring about a practical unity of purpose than one that tries to impose rigid disciplines.

The experience of France and Italy demonstrates what the European Monetary System can mean in practice. Officials in both countries bear witness to the fact that their governments' desire to remain full members of the system meant that they were able to use the realignment of March 1983 to introduce policies to bring inflation and budget deficits under control that would otherwise have been politically much more difficult. Moreover these policies were helped to get off to a good start by the EMS arrangements for mutual currency support, which deterred the foreign exchange markets from continued speculation against the franc and the lira after the realignment, thereby easing the inflationary pressures on the French and Italian economies. The subsequent success of the policies provides a vivid example of how the European dimension can enhance the effective capacity of national governments to take action in their own interest.

Most of those involved in the management of European economies would also share the view that, in the light of fluctuations in the value of the dollar and other external events, the EMS has helped to provide its participants with a remarkable degree of exchange rate stability. In May 1985 Helmut Schmidt put it thus:

The EMS, with its built-in psychological and political impetus towards the implementation of agreed stabilization policies, has succeeded in tuning down the volatilities of European exchange rates. Compared with the exchange rate fluctuations in the earlier 'Snake' between 1973 and 1978 as well as with the fluctuations against the free-floating currencies (especially the dollar), the exchange rates within the EMS have been rather stable. The average volatility of exchange rates was cut by half compared with the former period or compared with the fluctuations of the dollar and of sterling.[25]

To the extent, therefore, that European governments can agree on how to confront their problems – and nothing can be accomplished without that – the EMS procedures have demonstrated their usefulness in helping them work towards their objectives.

There is one final point concerning the internal affairs of the Community that deserves attention: its impact on long-standing communal and minority problems such as those of Northern Ireland, Belgium, Corsica and the Italian Tyrol, different as each of these is from the rest. When Britain and Ireland joined the EEC in 1973 the hope was sometimes expressed that Europe would in some never-defined way help to bring about a solution in Ulster. As in the other cases this has not proved to be so.

Yet the spirit of reconciliation that lies at the heart of the Community ideal has not been entirely without impact in Northern Ireland. I found on my annual visits as a Vice-President that it was possible to gather together a wider range of Northern Ireland opinion at a Community event, and to exchange views simultaneously with all those present, than was apparently possible in any other circumstance. A memorable example occurred on 27 January 1983 when I hosted a dinner at the Queen's University of Belfast, to celebrate the tenth anniversary of British, Irish and Danish entry, which was attended by representatives of every shade of non-violent opinion. Ted Heath as the British Prime Minister who had taken the country in, and Garret Fitzgerald, the Irish Prime Minister, both spoke. It was the first time since partition that a Prime Minister from Dublin had made a public speech on Northern Irish soil. All of us invoked the example of Franco-German reconciliation and it seemed not too much to hope that one day Catholics and Protestants in that small corner of Europe might be able to achieve as much. On a day-to-day level it has also been impressive to see how Northern Ireland's three representatives in the European Parliament, John Hume, the Reverend Ian Paisley and John Taylor, have so often been able to pursue the Province's interests there in a manner made the more effective by the absence of sectarian squabbles.

The External Record

The external activities of the Community, like the domestic ones, present an uneven picture. In some respects the Community can be said to operate very much as an entity; in others less so.

As a corollary of the internal customs union the Community has a common customs tariff which in turn led to its being endowed with the main responsibility for the external trade policy of its member states. On their behalf it negotiates international trading rules, draws up customs procedures, franchises and import quotas and, within the framework of international law, tries to ensure protection against unfair foreign competition. When trade agreements with third countries have to be negotiated, it is the Commission which does so on the basis of a mandate drawn up in the Council of Ministers. When international trade negotiations take place in the context of the GATT, it is again the Commission which deals with the rest of the world on the Community's behalf. When the big four meet informally, as they frequently do, those involved are the Special Trade Representative of the President of the United States, the relevant ministers from Japan and Canada and the member of the Commission responsible for external trade.

The Community also has its own development policy administered by the Commission. The development of the African continent is mentioned as one of Europe's vital tasks in the original Schuman Declaration. During the final stages of the negotiations for the Treaty of Rome the French, in order to mobilize the resources of other European countries for their colonial territories, insisted that the Community should have a development policy. When the British joined in 1973 the arrangements, which had meanwhile been adjusted to take account of the changes from colonial status to independence, were extended to benefit their ex-colonies and now they cover Portuguese- and Spanish-speaking territories as well.

The Community's policy is distinct from that of the member states rather than auxiliary to it and involves an annual expenditure of about 10 per cent of the total spent by those states themselves. Its most important element is the Lomé Convention, a far-reaching agreement covering aid, trade and the stabilization of export earnings with sixty-five countries in Africa, the Caribbean and the Pacific, usually referred to generically as the ACP. It is the direct descendant, much modernized and adapted, of the original French-inspired arrangements and regarded with some envy by other developing countries as well as by those, in other parts of the world, that are beyond that stage. When I represented the Commission at a conference with the members of the Association of South-East Asian Nations (ASEAN) in

Kuala Lumpur in 1983, Malaysian ministers suggested that it was a form of discrimination against their group that they did not enjoy similar privileges. In fact the Lomé arrangements would not be suitable for ASEAN, and co-operative agreements have been signed with that group and others in Latin America and the Mediterranean. It is true, however, that, like everything else done since Lomé was conceived, they are not as ambitious as the original.

None the less it can be said that the Community as such acts as an entity in international trade and aid matters. This is a notable achievement and nothing comparable exists anywhere else in the world. For a variety of reasons, though, this achievement does not inspire the sense of solidarity and common endeavour among the citizens of the member states that might have been expected. Governments invariably have great difficulty in sinking their differences in the search for a joint position and a mandate on which the Commission can act on the Community's behalf. Consequently, when ministers return home and have to face special interests complaining that their points of concern have not been adequately safeguarded, their natural reaction is to blame the Community for the shortcoming rather than to defend the agreement. Similarly, when they travel abroad and their opposite number in Washington, Tokyo or wherever it may be complains about a Community position, member state ministers often like to leave the impression that they would have adopted a much more 'reasonable' one if only the Community would have allowed them to do so.

The system has another and more serious fault arising from a common challenge commonly perceived as being the most effective spur to unity. In this area of policy that tends to mean that the Commission and the Council of Ministers have a built-in sympathy for those seeking protection from foreign competition even when the interests of the consumers ought to be paramount. This is liable to be especially so when those seeking the protection claim that its purpose is to give a rival European product time to get established or a European industry time to reform. In February 1983, for example, as part of a wider deal the Commission prevailed on the Japanese to limit their sales of videotape recorders in the Community. It was thought that this would enable the Dutch Philips and German Grundig substantially to increase sales of their own varieties of this product as well as enabling them to maintain prices at a higher level than would otherwise have been possible. Even with this help the European designs could not win, and a year later Philips announced that it would be introducing models developed in Japan. The Japanese meanwhile had benefited from higher margins on lower volume while the European consumer had lost out through higher prices and short supplies of the most popular models.

The Community's roles in respect of trade and aid both date from its earliest days. Only after it had been going for some time did the attempt begin to co-ordinate the foreign policies as such of the member states through the procedure known as Political Co-operation, or PoCo in Brussels jargon. Strictly speaking, Political Co-operation is separate and distinct from the Community as such and the normal Community rules do not apply to its procedures. But in order to be involved in Political Co-operation it is necessary to be a member of the Community, and experience has shown that if it is to be anything more than just another talking shop it has to be able to invoke Community instruments. The Community response to the Argentinian invasion of the Falkland Islands in April 1982 demonstrates this in an unmistakable way as well as showing how much the concept of the member states sticking together in a practical fashion developed during the 1970s and early 1980s, despite all their internal disagreements.

When the invasion occurred and Britain called on her partners to rally round, memories in Brussels and some other capitals, notably The Hague, went back to the Yom Kippur War of 1973 and the oil crisis that followed it. At that time the Dutch displayed more sympathy with Israel than most other Europeans as a result of which Holland became a particular object of Arab hostility and was subjected to an oil boycott. In the moment of crisis Community solidarity counted for nothing. Britain and France scrabbled all over the Gulf to make special deals with the suppliers and it was left to the much maligned multi-national oil companies to make sure that the Dutch and others without special influence in the Middle East were all right.

In the spring of 1982 Britain was already in a lonely position in the Community because of the long-running and rancorous row over budget contributions. There was also widespread unease on the Continent about the way the Falklands issue had been handled and above all about the dispatch of the Task Force. We wondered, therefore, how the other member states would respond to London's appeal and how the Community would emerge from the crisis by comparison with 1973-4.

From the outset the change was marked. To begin with, both in Britain and in other countries the general public simply assumed that at such a moment rallying round was the natural thing to do. In Italy, from where a high proportion of the Argentinian people originate, and in Ireland with its long and painful historical relationship with Britain, this assumption was, it is true, overlaid by other emotions. None the less the contrast with 1973-4 was striking, particularly as the oil crisis had threatened the whole of Europe while only Britain had interests directly at stake in the Falklands. As I participated in the Commission discussion on the statement to be issued condemning the invasion and on the British request for trade sanctions against Argentina, and listened to my French, German, Greek and other colleagues try to find the most helpful form of words and the speediest way to respond, I reflected on how different this was from the loquacious but disunited response of the Latin American countries.

Public sympathy and statements of support from heads of government and bodies such as the Commission are all very well, but fine words butter no parsnips. It was the request for trade sanctions which lay at the heart of the matter and which shows why the powers vested in the Community give it such an unusual capacity for action when the political will to undertake it exists. Under Article 113 of the Treaty of Rome the Council of Ministers, acting on a proposal from the Commission, could swiftly adopt a regulation suspending all imports from Argentina that had legally binding force in all member states. It would have been impossible to secure a similarly speedy and comprehensive result involving a whole group of countries acting simultaneously other than by what amounts to a joint law-making procedure. The regulation was subsequently twice extended with Italy and Ireland (under Article 224 of the Treaty) abstaining from applying the measures during the last month, while promising not to undermine them.

During their later stages the sanctions got caught up with the continuing row over the British budget contribution and lost some of their political shine in Britain. But they made a profound impression in Argentina, helped to heighten the Junta's sense of isolation, and showed in the clearest possible terms the interconnection between the fine words and supportive statements that countries can so easily make when their friends are in trouble and the hard action of which the Community, on the basis of its own, rather than national, procedures is capable.

This is a spectacular example of how effective the Community can be. It is also a highly unusual one. On too many other occasions the Community has either moved too slowly or hardly been able to respond at all, so that the effect of an external crisis has been to highlight differences between the member states and draw attention to the disparity that exists between the aspirations held on the Community's behalf and the reality.

The response to the imposition of martial law in Poland in December 1981 provides an example of too slow a response. From the moment Marshal Jaruzelski clamped down on the Solidarity union movement while Chancellor Schmidt was on an official visit to East Germany, it was clear that the Federal Republic's response would not be the same as that of many other Europeans. Bonn was cautious, anxious to avoid provoking a row with the Soviet Union, and doubtful in any case about how useful the imposition of trade sanctions on that country would be in helping those within Poland who were trying to liberalize Polish society from within and weaken their country's links with Moscow. Elsewhere there was a widespread desire to react dramatically to the Soviet-inspired clampdown and 'to do something about it'. As a result the Community was thrown into disarray and during the early months of 1982 the crisis in Poland served to expose differences between the member states rather than to demonstrate a common resolve between them. When those differences between Germany and its partners were finally bridged and regulations to limit imports from the Soviet Union agreed in mid-March, Greece – which could not even accept the principle that events in Poland should affect the Ten's relations with the Soviet Union – was excluded from their application.

If Poland provides an example of too slow a response, the Community's reaction to the shooting down of the Korean airliner by Soviet fighters in September 1983 shows how sometimes it can barely react at all. As it happened, Greece was holding the six-monthly rotating presidency at the time, so that the Greek Foreign Minister, Yiannis Haralambopoulos, was in the chair when the Foreign Ministers met to discuss the matter. With his clear eyes, flowing hair, luxurious moustache and erect figure, he looks like the partisan hero in the *Guns of Navarone* forty years on, and is in fact a considerable hero himself, having withstood torture and solitary confinement under the colonels without giving way. But, notwithstanding his personal record in defence of liberty and against oppression, it was the policy of the Greek Socialist government not to offend the Soviet Union. He therefore began by trying to prevent a proper discussion of the atrocity from taking place, and when it became apparent that the others would insist on some sort of condemnation of the Soviet action emerging from the meeting, he ensured that it would be at the point of the lowest common denominator.

Over the Falklands, Poland and the Korean airliner, the Community had to operate in the glare of massive media attention. It is when it is out of the limelight and involved in a continuous negotiation of the sort that enables diplomats and ministers to follow a consistent line of policy and build on what has gone before that the system of Political Co-operation works best. Its first major success was in the preparation for the opening of the Conference on Security and Co-operation in Europe (CSCE) in 1973. Thereafter, on the long march from Helsinki where the original conference took place to Belgrade and Madrid where follow-up meetings were held, the Community countries maintained a common approach and provided the motor for policy development on the Western side. Without this solid core it is highly unlikely that such a high degree of Western solidarity could have been sustained or that the success, limited though it may be, that has been achieved in the negotiations could have been secured.

For outsiders as well as for those within the Community the crucial problem is to know when the member states intend to operate as a group and wish to be seen as such and when they wish to be considered as individual countries. At one moment it seems to be the former and at the next the latter. And sometimes they are caught on the hop and need time to make up their minds, as happened in the spring of 1985 when they were confronted with the problem of how to respond to President Reagan's suggestion that Europeans should participate in the research phase for the Strategic Defence Initiative (SDI), or 'Star Wars' as it is often called.

This brings us to the one major issue from which the Community has been absent since the outset and in which there is no distinctive European voice, namely security and defence. It was not always so. When the foundations of contemporary European co-operation were being laid in the post-war years, such founding fathers as Jean Monnet and Paul Henri Spaak, who ended his political career as secretary-general of NATO, were equally concerned with both. The abortive attempt to form a European Defence Community occurred soon after the formation of the European Coal and Steel Community and its failure was one of the factors that spurred governments on in their subsequent negotiations to create the European Economic Community.

Only after that did defence and security on the one hand and economic and foreign policy on the other come to be regarded as falling into different categories. In the 1970s the division was rigidly adhered to, especially by the French. In 1977, when the Dutch commissioner and former Defence Minister Henk Vredeling suggested in a Commission meeting that naval units from the member states should be used to police and enforce the fishing policy then under discussion, and that it would provide a useful precedent for breaking down the barrier between his old responsibilities and his current ones, the French commissioners reacted with horror. In 1981 I made a speech at St Andrews University advocating that member states should seek ways of co-operating in defence procurement and of linking their activities in the security and foreign policy fields. My Irish colleague, the former Foreign Minister Michael O'Kennedy, was so outraged that he summoned the press to denounce my suggestions.

Since then the mood has changed. When the heads of government meet in the European Council, the line between security and other matters is sometimes completely forgotten in their intimate exchanges, and it can be blurred a good deal in Political Co-operation meetings as well. In fact, after the one in September 1983 which discussed the shooting down of the Korean airliner, Mr Haralambopoulos further enraged his colleagues by revealing that they had also discussed the deployment of American missiles in Germany. He thereby simultaneously embarrassed the German minister because of the sensitivity of the subject at that time in the Federal Republic, the Irish minister because of Irish public opinion's perennial worry that membership of the Community might conflict with their policy of neutrality and the Danish minister because of Danish public opinion's hostility to anything happening in a Community context that falls outside the strict confines of the Treaty of Rome.

Nowhere has the mood in these matters moved on more than in Paris, where interest in encouraging defence and security co-operation among European countries has been receiving increasing attention in recent years. Yet it is not in the Community context that the French have suggested this question should be explored. In a move backed by the Belgians, which provides yet another illustration of how flexible the European idea has become, they suggested in 1984 that the appropriate forum would be the long-dormant Western European Union, which happens to include all countries which at that time belonged to the Community, minus Ireland, Greece and Denmark; a manoeuvre clearly designed to enable the majority to go ahead without forcing the minority to oppose them.

This episode encapsulates the reasons why Europe exists on so many different planes, why it is so difficult to describe and why the countries that go to make it up cannot be forced into a uniform mould. The Community and the whole concept of European co-operation are based on the idea expressed by the Belgian national motto: 'L'union fait la force', 'Union makes strength.' At the same time it must take account of the Luxembourg motto: 'Mir woelle bleiwe wat mir sin', 'We want to remain what we are.' That sentiment too has to be respected and it is to an examination of its causes and implications that we now turn.

2

The Reasons for Reality

On 29 March 1982 'the great and the good' from all over Europe drove through the Brussels fog to the Palais des Académies to celebrate the twenty-fifth anniversary of the signing of the Treaty of Rome. We all sat on little gilt chairs – except for the King of the Belgians and President Mitterrand who, as the only heads of state present, had special more throne-like seats – and listened to speeches by the Presidents of the European Parliament, the Commission, the Court of Justice and the Council of Ministers, in that order. It was a Community occasion and they were supposed to be the stars. But outside that room few would have been able to name let alone recognize them and it was the heads of state and government who attracted all the attention, just as they would have done in any other gathering.

Nothing in the Community ever starts on time and as we waited for the proceedings to begin one noticed that President Mitterrand, although less than a year in office, had already acquired that aura of unapproachability so characteristic of French Presidents as he held himself slightly aloof from the exchanges of greetings and reminiscences going on around him. Mrs Thatcher wore black and looked forbidding, her mind no doubt already on the next round of the Great British Budget

Battle due to begin that afternoon when the European Council assembled. Chancellor Schmidt, as usual on ceremonial occasions, was obviously impatient with all the fuss, but forbore from the habit of vacuuming snuff off the back of his hand, like an industrial cleaner, with which he can so easily disconcert any gathering. Mitterrand, Schmidt and Mrs Thatcher are all rather small of stature and it seemed appropriate to the occasion that the 6 ft 5 in frame of the last remaining signatory of the Treaty still holding high public office, the former Dutch Foreign Minister and then secretary-general of NATO, Joseph Luns, should tower over them. The speeches were mostly poor, looking back to the good old days and presenting few broad perspectives of the future. Afterwards, as we all trooped across the road to the Royal Palace for lunch, I could not help reflecting upon the uninspiring nature of the whole affair. The drizzle, which had replaced the fog, seemed to provide a fitting finale.

The following day the flags raised to mark the anniversary were lowered to half-mast as the news came through of the death of Walter Hallstein, the German who, as the first President of the Commission, had done so much to mould its early character and aspirations. He had been a high priest of the supranational ideal and infuriated General de Gaulle, who felt:

He had made Brussels, where he resided, into a sort of capital. There he sat, surrounded by all the trappings of sovereignty, directing his colleagues, allocating jobs among them, controlling several thousand officials who were appointed, promoted and remunerated at his discretion, receiving the credentials of foreign ambassadors, laying claim to high honours on the occasion of his official visits, concerned above all to further the amalgamation of the Six, believing that the pressure of events would bring about what he envisaged.[1]

To have inspired such a passage from the General's pen, Hallstein must have been a formidable man. However, there was no doubt which of their respective visions of how Europe should develop had triumphed. The symbolism inherent in the timing of Hallstein's death seemed unmistakable and attracted widespread comment. It was as if an ideal as well as a man was being declared dead.

Two Concepts

Federalism and inter-governmentalism, supranationalism and co-operation between different nationalities: two different concepts of Europe known by a variety of different names have been vying with each other since the earliest days of the Community. In their wisdom, and as a result of a characteristic Community compromise, the founding fathers allowed neither to prevail in the Treaty of Rome, which represents a delicate balance between the two.

In the earlier phase when the European Coal and Steel Community was formed and the European Defence Community conceived, the federalists were in the ascendant. Within the clearly defined sphere of the ECSC the transfer of sovereignty was substantial, with immense decision-making powers being vested in the High Authority established to run the enterprise. Even then, though, the Council of Ministers retained important levers of control, including in some cases the power of veto. No sooner was the ECSC operational than plans were launched, in the context of the need to rearm West Germany and to strengthen the Western Alliance, for the European Defence Community. Close on its heels came the idea for a Political Community to encompass and guide it. Preparatory work on the Political Community was entrusted to an *ad hoc* assembly which produced a document that, in Monnet's eyes, 'provided for simultaneous steps towards a full federal structure'.[2] But the Defence Community proposal was defeated in the French National Assembly on 30 August 1954, and that for a Political Community died with it. Thereafter the federalist tide began to turn. When the discussions that were to lead to the establishment of the EEC got under way at Messina in Sicily, of whose university the then Italian Foreign Minister, Gaetano Martino, was rector, the inter-governmental view was gathering momentum. In the final text of the Treaty of Rome the two are skilfully blended.

For the inter-governmentalists the key point was the decision-making power vested in the Council of Ministers. The new Commission was given far less capacity in this respect than the old High Authority, as well as a less resounding name. Everything important had to be settled by the Council, which being made up of ministers from national governments is in effect an extension of those governments. The inter-governmentalists were determined that it should forever dominate the new creation. For the federalists hope resided in the Commission.

It was given the sole right to submit proposals to the Council – the 'unique right of initiative' in Community jargon – as well as responsibility for implementing the Council's decisions, and ensuring that the member states fulfilled their undertakings. The federalists saw it as an embryo federal government, and hoped these attributes would enable it, over time, to become one. They hoped that as the impetus of economic integration gathered momentum more and more material interests would gather round the Community, thereby enhancing the Commission's role at the expense of the Council and of national governments, and making it an ever more central and important instrument in the evolution and conduct of policies on a Europe-wide basis. Over time, according to this line of reasoning, the Council would evolve into a sort of Chamber of States, or Senate, which would in turn be matched by a House of Representatives in the form of the European Parliament. At the outset that body was given the power to censure and dismiss the Commission as well as the right to be consulted on its proposals, and it was thought that after it had become directly elected wide-ranging new powers would be accorded to it. Between them the Parliament and Commission, to the plaudits of public opinion, would drive their way through the defences of the nationalists to the creation of a federal Europe.

On one point all could agree. The Community represented a unique structure which could not be related to any known models of government, nor to any conventional theory of inter-state relations. As Andrew Shonfield subsequently put it in the title of his 1972 Reith Lectures, it represented the start of 'A Journey to an Unknown Destination'.

Public opinion, however, cannot be roused by such a concept. Whatever the small print and counterbalancing clauses of the Treaty might say, the creation of the Community was widely seen as a first step towards the fulfilment of the federalist dream of a United States of Europe. It was the federalists who provided it with its moral inspiration and established the tone and style of the rhetoric that have surrounded it to this day. These in turn embedded in the public mind the scale of values and criteria for measuring progress by which it has to a great degree since been judged.

At a time when there was a universal awareness of the extremes to which nationalism could lead, and when the states were still struggling to recover the moral authority they had lost in the humiliations of the war and the anarchy that followed it, federalism appeared as an attractive alternative to old and discredited notions. It seemed the wave of the future. It was also part of the intellectual heritage of the resistance movements. All over continental Europe many of those who had been in the forefront of the struggle against Nazism and Fascism had been inspired by the vision of a 'federal union of all European countries from the Atlantic to and including Poland', as the German exile in Holland, Hans Dieter Salinger, wrote in *Die Wiedergeburt von Europa*. In 1941 the French resistance leader Henri Frenay had written in his underground news-sheet, *Les Petites Ailes*, 'What we want in Europe is a federation of equal states with Germany cured of her megalomania.' In the same year a group of Italian opponents of Mussolini imprisoned on the island of Ventotene produced 'The Ventotene Manifesto', which called for a federation to abolish 'the division of Europe into nation states'. Among those who drafted it was Altiero Spinelli, the future commissioner and, more recently, the inspiration behind the European Parliament's 1984 proposal for a 'Draft Treaty establishing the European Union'.[3]

The supranational ideal that lies at the heart of federalism is a generous one. It aspires to the overcoming of ancient rivalries and the reconciliation of previously warring peoples. When faced with its propositions, as with those of Quakerism, it is natural to respond with words such as 'If only it was practical I would love to support it' or 'If only the world was ripe for such an approach it would have my support'. When the Community began there were many, like Leo Tindemans, who believed that 'the old Adam of nationalism had been banished for ever',[4] that the supranational ideal was practical and that the world, or at any rate Europe, was ripe for it. The young were inspired by the vision it held out, while to many of the old the Treaty seemed 'a new phenomenon in the political and moral world and an astonishing victory gained by enlightened reason over brute force', as George Washington once said of the American constitution.[5]

The importance of these considerations should not be underestimated. They enabled the Community institutions to begin life with considerable moral authority and helped to establish a willingness on the part of member states to sink differences and overcome problems that those who know only the Community of the 1970s and 1980s look back on with envy. Without the imagination and determination of the federalists the Community would never have been established. Without the impetus and energy that their ideals created, its structure would never have taken root.

The Decline of Federalism

But for all that the federal ideal could never have endured as a guide and stimulus to political action. Like the bloom of youth it was bound to fade. De Gaulle and history were lying in wait. President Mitterrand has written in another context of 'The stubborn presence of the centuries. Only the unwise hope to escape it.'⁶ Nowhere is that more true than of Europe, the states that go to make it up and the relations between them.

General de Gaulle and his supporters had consistently opposed all the great post-war European initiatives: the European Coal and Steel Community, the European Defence Community and the European Economic Community. When the ratification of the Treaty of Rome was being debated in the National Assembly the Gaullist deputy Raymond Triboulet called on his colleagues to vote against 'the Europe of Jean Monnet', and they responded. None the less when the General returned to power in 1958 his government decided to hold to France's commitments and to implement the treaties. They saw the value of the basic bargain that had been struck with Germany and the opportunities it provided for France; they appreciated the prospective benefits for French agriculture and they thought that French industry too could gain from a measure of liberalization after years of stifling protectionism.

Above all at the deepest personal and political level the General was impressed by the German Chancellor, Konrad Adenauer, 'of all Germans the most capable and the most willing to commit his country alongside France'. For their first and crucial meeting as heads of government the General felt that 'the atmosphere of a family home would be more striking than the splendour of a palace as a setting for the historic encounter between this old Frenchman and this very old German in the name of their two peoples. And so my wife and I offered the Chancellor the modest hospitality of La Boissière', their house at Colombey-les-Deux-Eglises. The conversation between the two men ranged wide and deep and laid the basis for their subsequent constructive partnership. 'We discussed Europe at length,' the General later recorded. 'Adenauer agreed with me that there could be no question of submerging the identity of our two nations in a stateless institution.'[7]

So, notwithstanding the upheavals in France, the new Community institutions set to work.[8] The Treaty with its detailed instructions and deadlines for action provided a clear programme to which all had subscribed. Agreements did not always fall into place easily; indeed 'stopping the clock' to provide more time for negotiation became a cliché of Brussels life, but they were reached and the framework of the Common Agricultural Policy and the Common Market began to take shape. From all over the world companies flocked to Brussels to establish offices in order to be in on the ground floor of a new politico-economic construction and the opportunities expected to flow from it. In Shelley's words, 'The great morning of the world when first God dawned on chaos' seemed to have arrived.

By mid-1961 the progress was so impressive that Britain –

which had boycotted the European Coal and Steel Community, stood aloof from the European Defence Community and tried to sabotage the European Economic Community with its proposal for a free trade area – was applying to join. In British government and establishment circles at least the doubts about the trustworthiness of the French and Germans and the capacity of continentals to organize durable ventures, which had been so widespread a decade earlier, had been largely cast aside. In their place was a growing fear that Europe would be organized by a Franco-German combination to the exclusion of Britain and to the detriment of her interests. The Community was perceived as something that worked and membership of it as being essential if Britain was to maintain her international economic and political interests. That in itself constituted something of a triumph for the Community, and though de Gaulle's veto of the British application, delivered at a memorable press conference in January 1963, disappointed many throughout the Six it did not interfere with the work in progress towards fulfilling the Treaty programme.

The clash came in 1965 when the Commission coupled its proposals for the final implementation of the CAP with plans for it to be financed by special Community 'own resources' that would be subject to control by the European Parliament, the most avowedly supranational of all the institutions. When he realized that his partners were prepared to go along with these ideas de Gaulle reacted violently and instituted a virtual boycott of Community proceedings in what became known as the 'empty chair' crisis. His position was clear. On the one hand the Commission must give up all idea of acting as a European government-in-waiting and of attempting to impose its will on the member states. On the other the Treaty requirement that the Council of Ministers should, in a variety of prescribed circumstances, resolve differences through majority voting should not apply where the vital interests of a member state were at stake.

The row was finally settled with the famous 'Luxembourg compromise' of January 1966. In the interests of getting the CAP fully under way France gave up a good deal. Even the principle, enunciated by the French, that if faced with a statement by a member state that one of its vital interests was at stake the others would not press the issue to a vote was not explicitly endorsed by the rest. None the less this row marked the moment at which the supremacy of the inter-governmental over the federal approach was established. The Treaty remained an ambiguous compromise, but thereafter it gradually became clear that the Community would evolve as a union of sovereign states or not at all. The alternative option of those states relinquishing sovereignty to supranational institutions became an increasingly dead letter.

This was not immediately apparent at the time. Work on the Treaty programme continued and the Commission achieved a formidable triumph as the sole negotiator for the Community in the Kennedy Round of GATT negotiations. When Pompidou succeeded de Gaulle the enlargement issue was finally unblocked, and Britain, Ireland and Denmark* at last joined on 1 January 1973. As part of an overall settlement the Community was also given its own financial resources,† and some powers over them were accorded to the European Parliament, though the arrangements were more modest than those to which de Gaulle had objected. In December 1969 the Summit at The

* Negotiations were also successfully completed with Norway, but at a referendum the Norwegian people decided not to join.
† The system was to have been introduced gradually between 1971 and 1975. As a result of successive delays it came into force only on 1 January 1979.

Hague laid down the objective of economic and monetary union, and the Luxembourg Prime Minister, Pierre Werner, and the Vice-President of the Commission and future French Prime Minister, Raymond Barre, produced a plan to achieve it.

At the Paris Summit of October 1972, called to prepare the way for the new enlarged Community, the heads of state and government of the Six and of the incoming members pledged themselves to fulfil Werner's and Barre's ambition by the end of 1980 as part of a transformation of 'the whole complex of the relations of member states into a European Union'[9] – language reminiscent of that heard in 1985 in the run-up to the Spanish and Portuguese accession. They also undertook to set up a new regional development fund to correct 'the structural and regional imbalances which might affect the realisation of economic and monetary union',[10] and committed themselves to an ambitious set of objectives in the social, industrial, energy and other fields.

But the Werner Plan, as it became known, never really got off the ground and, as was pointed out in the preceding chapter, the impressive schemes to build up an array of other spending policies around the CAP yielded small results. Meanwhile the existence of the Luxembourg compromise came to exert a decisive influence over the working practices of the Community and prevented progress on even the most minor issues. Consensus became the acknowledged requirement on virtually all matters, even those where the Treaty envisaged votes and where no one could sensibly claim that vital national interests were at stake. If consensus was not forthcoming, decisions were simply postponed so that by the late 1970s it was only in the annual budget procedure that votes took place as a matter of normal routine. On one occasion when the French were in a minority of one they threatened to invoke the compromise even there. A number of smaller countries immediately changed sides in the argument. When I asked the Belgian minister why, he replied, 'To prevent the French from using the veto and so to preserve the practice of majority voting in this field at least.'

Not until 18 May 1982 was the supremacy of the Luxembourg compromise finally challenged when the British, after voting for all the component parts of an agricultural prices settlement, proclaimed a vital national interest in an attempt to hold up its implementation as a manoeuvre designed to help them in negotiations going on at the same time over their budgetary contribution. In the preceding days they received warnings from several quarters, including myself, that the tactic would misfire; the other countries would not accept such a tangential use of the compromise to prevent a decision that all of them wished to take. The British went ahead nevertheless and to their fury found themselves disregarded and the prices settlement adopted by a majority vote.

As the 1970s progressed it became clear that the Community would not develop on a primarily institutional basis with the Commission and Parliament driving all before them on the march towards a federal Europe. Majority voting apart, the institutions could in general ensure that the member states honoured their Treaty commitments. The edifice constructed in the 1960s was held in place and a few new pediments and balconies were added. But if anything new was to be done the heads of state and government had to be directly and actively involved. When Roy Jenkins, as President of the Commission, relaunched the idea of economic and monetary union in the autumn of 1977 and engaged the interest and support of President Giscard d'Estaing and Chancellor Schmidt it was carried into effect, on a modified basis, as the European Monetary System (EMS). When they could not reach agreement, as was for long the case over the British budget problem, no amount of negotiation in the Council of Ministers, brainstorming by the Commission or interventions by the Parliament could fill the vacuum.

The Community's misfortune is that while those involved in running the machine have been aware of the realities for many years and conducted themselves accordingly, the rhetoric, images and objectives of the supranational ideal have continued to dominate its language. In speeches, communiqués, reports, public utterances and plans of every kind the impression is constantly given that federal union remains the one true faith with anything else some form of aberration or human frailty, understandable perhaps but to be resisted. Gaston Thorn's final speech as President of the Commission to the European Parliament in December 1984 is a classic example of this genre, but far from unique. He said then that 'to be in favour of inter-governmental co-operation is – as the proponents themselves should openly admit – to be against the Community'.[11] The result is that the language and actions of the Community and of the member states diverge increasingly, like those of a Victorian mill-owner's prayers on a Sunday and his actions during the rest of the week.

No new intellectual or moral framework has been constructed to enable the general public to make sense of what is going on and no new objectives have been set with which they can identify and towards which they can aspire. This is the great lacuna at the heart of the Community. It explains why attitudes in its institutions should so often either appear to be theoretical and unworldly, or bring to mind Carlyle's typical Victorian intellectual, 'devoid of faith and terrified of scepticism'.

When individuals try to break out of a dead end they all too often look for a scapegoat on to whose shoulders they can heap the blame for their own disappointed hopes. In the 1960s it was de Gaulle, in the late 1970s and early 1980s Mrs Thatcher. Both certainly played important roles, one of which I have already discussed and to the other I will turn shortly. They left a strong personal impress on the rows in which they were engaged and this in turn generated widespread and deep personal animosity. But even with their strong personalities they could not single-handedly have changed the whole direction in which the Community was going. Like all political leaders they reflect as well as form the environment in which they operate. The reason why the Community is as it is and European co-operation has developed as it has is the result of the interaction of a number of complex factors. Much of the rest of this book will be devoted to analysing their origins and effects, but now is the moment briefly to summarize them.

One factor certainly is 'the stubborn presence of the centuries'. As the memories of war and post-war began to recede so the authority of the nation state began to reassert itself. Far from disappearing, national pride and national identity once again had to be reckoned with and the interests of the nation states and their governments were confirmed as the pre-eminent political force in Europe. As far as the Community was concerned this trend was accentuated by the arrival of Britain, Ireland and Denmark, three countries untouched by the early idealism and with strong national personalities. Enlargement also had two other consequences. It widened the range of difference between the underlying situations of the member states and increased the probable variation to be found at any one time in the political views of the elected governments. The combination of these three factors would in any circumstances have made the decision-making process more difficult.

It has been further complicated by another one, which receives less attention than it should, namely the nature of modern politics. To a large degree this is a process in which governments are engaged in a ceaseless struggle to reconcile conflicting and often mutually incompatible demands from the special interest groups that go to make up their electorates, a struggle that must always be carried on in the full glare of publicity. The deals and compromises to which it gives rise are invariably such as to inhibit the governments' scope to trade prospective gains in one area for possible losses in another at the European level. This is true even of the most enthusiastically 'pro-European' administrations. The recession leading to the run-down of basic industries and high unemployment has, by exacerbating social tensions within the member states, made the problem worse. Not surprisingly in view of all this, the way in which the existing common policies, notably but not only the CAP, worked out in practice became a source of mounting disillusion during the 1970s and early 1980s. The political bargaining process by which they are run, buffeted this way and that by conflicting pressures, was revealed all too starkly as an inefficient way of setting priorities and allocating scarce resources.

Finally the idea of large-scale European policies came to seem outmoded in intellectual terms. Their blueprints were drawn up when there was great faith in the merits and advantages of sheer scale, in industry and other walks of life as well as in politics. It was matched by a belief in the capacity of wise, well-intentioned, well-informed public servants to identify the public interest, to produce prosperity for all and to overcome political and economic problems as well as those left over by history. It had seemed natural to transfer the concepts of national planning, which had worked so well in France with Monnet playing a prominent role,* to the European level. The future seemed to lie with the big battalions. As opinion in the member states turned against those ideas so their European version lost credibility as well.

All these factors have their roots in the individual member states. It is to these, therefore, rather than to the institutions that one must turn in order to form a view of the possibilities open to the Community and the constraints upon it.

France

The place to start is Paris, the operational base of Monnet, Schuman and de Gaulle. The French as individuals and France as a country have done more to influence the construction of Community Europe than anyone else. Monnet's original conception; Schuman's Plan; de Gaulle's counter-view and impact; Pompidou's decision to reverse de Gaulle's veto and allow Britain in, accompanied by Ireland and Denmark; Giscard d'Estaing's launching with Schmidt of the European Monetary System; Mitterrand's role during the 1984 French presidency in resolving the British budget dispute after it had dominated the Community agenda for many years: all bear witness to that.

Most major international organizations – the United Nations, the International Monetary Fund, the World Bank, NATO *et al.* – owe their foundation principally to the United States and Britain as the leading Western allies at the end of the war and in the immediate post-war period. Their structures continue to bear a strong Anglo-Saxon imprint and, with the exception of the United Nations with its built-in Third World majority, the United States remains in every way the single most important member.

* Monnet was the first Planning Commissioner in France after the war, and the author of the idea for a Planning Commissariat.

The Community is different. The United States was not, of course, involved and Britain, by her own choice, was absent during its formative period. France was accordingly able to play the leading role without, at first, any serious rival. Alone among major international organizations the Community institutions do not operate primarily in English. French remains *la langue dominante* and their bureaucracy, in terms of structures and the titles accorded to individual *fonctionnaires*, derives unmistakably from French models. In the Commission French habits of thought are also very much in the ascendant.

From the very outset the French have tended to feel a rather proprietorial pride about the European enterprise in all its various forms, regardless of whether they happen to be part of the majority or an isolated minority on the question of the hour. In June 1950 that remarkable American journalist Janet Flanner, who wrote a regular letter from Paris for the *New Yorker* under the pseudonym of Genêt, was telling her readers, 'Most French citizens feel that the Schuman Plan, if made to work, could establish new Franco-German relations, a new spirit of Western union and, lastly, a new French prestige, which is what they usually mention first.' In November of the same year she was writing that the French feel that 'France has become once more the planning brain of Europe.'[12]

This has been true ever since. For the French, Europe is, in a certain sense, an extension of their own personality, an arena in which their country counts for more than in any other, and almost a ladder whereby others can become more like them. It has a unique place in their hearts, quite unlike any of their other external commitments. For this reason any serious contender for leadership in French politics must show that he has a vision of Europe and its future. In the run-up to the 1984 European elections, for instance, Mitterrand, Giscard d'Estaing and Barre all made major speeches on that theme, quite independently of their election activities, which were of an overwhelmingly domestic nature. Nothing remotely comparable was attempted by the party leaders in Britain, nor apparently expected.

The French want their government to play a prominent role in European affairs. When France assumes the six-monthly rotating presidency of the Council of Ministers they expect their own President to emerge as the arbiter of Europe, while he invariably wishes to secure a triumph that will enable him to appear so. For this reason I felt able to tell Geoffrey Howe, as Foreign Secretary, in December 1983 that, notwithstanding all the difficulties the French had made over the British budget problem, they would, while in the Chair during the first six months of 1984, make a determined effort to solve it. They duly did so, finally achieving success at the Fontainebleau European Council in June of that year.

However obdurate, self-serving and nationalistic a French position may be, they have no difficulty in presenting it as 'European' and conveying the impression that 'what's good for France is good for Europe and vice versa' because – like Mr 'Engine Charlie' Wilson, who coined the original adage in relation to General Motors and the United States – they really believe it. It would be a mistake to assume that this technique has ever enabled them to get away with the negotiating murder the British imagine, but it does yield tangible results. This is not simply because of the leadership role France has played for so long. It is also because others know that though the French will be prepared to stick to a position, regardless of the odds against them, till they feel they have secured the best possible result, when they do settle they will wish the agreement to be regarded thenceforth as a 'European' triumph and to become the new 'European' way of doing things. This gives them a decided advantage over the only other nation prepared single-handedly to defy everyone else, namely the British, who so often make the mistake of presenting their case in too nationalistic a way.

Their proprietorial attitude to Europe enables the French to redefine their own interest and Community orthodoxy with surprising speed when the need arises. For many years, while the British were demanding a rebate on the grounds that they paid too large a contribution into the Community budget, the French replied that as the Community had its 'own resources', which belonged to it as of right and were merely collected by the member states on its behalf, it was wrong to think in national terms at all. In 1983 Paris reached the conclusion that France was moving into a net deficit position and that under the prevailing rules its bill would rise substantially after the arrival of Spain and Portugal. Almost overnight the French began discussing budget problems on the basis of how to limit the demands on the so-called *deficitaire* countries. Other governments and some of my Commission colleagues could hardly believe their ears.

Nor do the French feel constrained by Community orthodoxy from suggesting forms of co-operation outside the Treaty framework. It is the British who have the reputation for pragmatism, but the French who practise it. Accordingly, if some form of industrial activity in conjunction with other countries is more likely to get off the ground on a bilateral basis untrammelled by Community rules, they will not hesitate to suggest it. Similarly, when they wished to encourage a more co-ordinated European approach to defence and security and wished to avoid problems with the Irish, Danes and Greeks, they suggested the resurrection of the Western European Union. If the British had made a similar proposal they would have run the risk of being accused of trying to undermine the Community. Because the French did so, it could be looked at on its merits.

Their proprietorial attitude towards Community and European affairs also leaves the French free to adopt what might be termed a 'negotiating' approach towards the Community's rules. When the Commission publishes its annual list of legal proceedings launched against the member states, France has recently been, with Italy, at the head of the list of those being sued. The French, however, are more adroit than the Italians in ensuring that matters are resolved before the European Court finally rules. By this means they are able to continue in their old ways for as long as possible and, quite frequently, to obtain useful last-minute concessions as well. In the case of steel, too, they took much longer than most to make the capacity cuts required by the crisis regime.

No nation combines idealism, sentiment and self-interest more effectively than the French and this is as true of their approach to Europe as anything else. The Community may have a special place in their hearts, but it is also the means by which they seek to achieve certain specific and permanent objectives. Basically these are two: influence with and, if possible, over Germany, and the reinforcement of France's own capacity to play an effective role in the world. Their manifestations change with circumstances and the particular priorities of whichever government happens to be in power in Paris; the relationship with Germany is an especially complex and evolving one. But these are the two objectives that run like a golden thread through French European policy.

The view that inspired French policy towards Germany for more than two centuries after the Peace of Westphalia in 1648 and cast its shadow into our own was spelt out by Adolphe Thiers in the French Chamber of Deputies in 1866. 'I beg

Table 4 Infringement proceedings opened or pursued by the Commission 1979–84, classified by member state and stage of proceedings

	1979	1980	1981	1982	1983	1984
Letter of Formal Notice						
Belgium	25	34	29	27	34	55
Denmark	10	14	21	16	13	21
France	23	34	39	68	55	92
W. Germany	15	15	22	26	16	36
Greece	—	—	—	8	26	60
Ireland	17	25	28	30	16	33
Italy	30	39	64	66	69	67
Luxembourg	24	26	17	30	24	28
Netherlands	19	21	16	32	16	28
UK	24	19	20	32	20	34
Reasoned Opinion						
Belgium	13	10	26	18	8	17
Denmark	3	2	6	10	3	3
France	10	10	22	33	21	29
W. Germany	7	3	14	15	8	13
Greece	—	—	—	2	4	27
Ireland	5	5	4	17	6	12
Italy	15	19	41	34	21	26
Luxembourg	6	5	19	8	2	6
Netherlands	9	7	7	16	3	5
UK	7	7	8	4	7	10
Reference to Court of Justice						
Belgium	4	8	9	8	4	4
Denmark	—	1	2	1	3	1
France	2	4	5	8	12	14
W. Germany	1	1	2	4	4	7
Greece	—	—	—	—	2	4
Ireland	1	1	3	3	1	3
Italy	7	11	20	14	12	12
Luxembourg	1	2	2	3	—	3
Netherlands	—	—	5	2	3	2
UK	2	—	2	2	1	4

the Germans to reflect,' he said, 'that the highest principle of European politics is that Germany shall be composed of independent states connected by only a slender federative thread. That was the principle proclaimed by all Europe at the Congress of Westphalia'[13] – a congress that confirmed and legitimized the atomization of Germany by recognizing the sovereignty of over 300 separate German states and largely depriving Germany of access to the sea. A union of Germany, Thiers added, would subvert the balance of power and endanger the peace of Europe. Four years later that union was achieved when France was defeated by Prussia and her allies in the war of 1870 and the German Empire was proclaimed at Versailles in January 1871. France lost territory in Alsace and Lorraine and was forced to pay substantial reparations as well.

After the First World War many Frenchmen would have liked to reduce Germany as far as possible back to the powerlessness of the Peace of Westphalia. The fact that by then Germany's population, manufacturing skill and resources were all greater than France's spurred Clemenceau on in his efforts to grind as much as he could out of the defeated enemy at the peace conference held at Versailles, the scene of the enemy's triumph half a century previously. De Gaulle subsequently argued that it was the 'Anglo-Saxons' who had denied France 'the fruits of victory' by stopping the war too soon, leaving 'the enemy's unity, territory and resources intact' and later forcing France to renounce reparations owed to her by Germany.[14] He was not alone in that view.

After the Second World War the United States, supported by Britain, was the dominant power in Western Europe. Even if the French wanted to – which some of them did – they could not have repeated the pattern that followed previous conflicts. None the less, the problem of how to control Germany and to prevent her recovery from again leading her to challenge France remained. It was in part to tackle this age-old problem that supremely practical French political leaders took up the ideas of that supremely practical idealist, Jean Monnet. If France could not be Germany's *Gauleiter*, she would instead be her guide, philosopher and friend on the road back to rehabilitation and respectability. Another reason was that they saw that if the economic and industrial potential of a renascent Germany could be harnessed to French political leadership, France's diplomatic scope would be enormously enhanced. With Europe as a base she could aspire to a real role in the world of the superpowers that would otherwise be beyond her.

The supreme act of Franco-German reconciliation and the basis ever since of the special relationship between the two countries within the context of the European Community is the Franco-German Treaty of 1963. The network of formal and regular consultations and meetings that it established provides a model of how institutional arrangements can over time transform two mutually suspicious and distrustful states into close working allies. The focal point is, of course, the frequent meetings between the two heads of government, which took on a special significance during the time when Giscard d'Estaing and Schmidt were in charge, because of their close personal friendship and their habit of talking to each other (in English) on the telephone. But that has never been more than the tip of an iceberg that extends far below the surface of the public relationship and is sustained by an equally deep sense of common interests. It is also buttressed by a closeness of working relationships between French and German officials far surpassing that between those of any other countries, including the Benelux.

Over the years the balance between France and Germany has

changed considerably. Germany long since outgrew the need for leading strings. It has become not simply the strongest European economy but by far the strongest. The hopes expressed in the 1970s by Giscard d'Estaing, by Herman Kahn in a noted Hudson Institute report and others, that France would move into the same league and perhaps even outstrip Germany in the 1980s, now look absurd. The question has become much more of when and in what manner the French will next need financial or economic support of one sort or another from across the Rhine. Germany is also the most powerful conventional military power in Europe and a privileged ally of the United States. France can provide no substitute for that.

Far from diminishing France's interest in the special relationship these changes enhance it. The stronger Germany is, the more vital it becomes for France that the two countries should not be at odds with each other and the truer it becomes that when they are at one they can carry everything in the Community before them – except Mrs Thatcher when she digs in. Indeed in the European context as a whole, if Paris and Bonn are in agreement on something it is well on the way to being accomplished. If they are not, no other combination has yet shown itself capable of achieving remotely similar results. For France, therefore, influence in Bonn remains of immense significance. As Germany's strength relative to that of France increases, harnessing it to French ends becomes more difficult and the effort required greater; disappointments have to be borne with a better grace than would once have been the case. But the prize in terms of what that strength can do to help France achieve her objectives grows correspondingly.

Normally it is France rather than Germany that has the greater number of active objectives to pursue in the Community. Partly this is because of the French attitudes already described which, as will shortly be shown, are not to be found in Germany. But there are, as one would expect, other reasons as well.

France has a strong centralized and *dirigiste* tradition deriving from Louis XIV's Minister of Finance, Jean Baptiste Colbert, and likes to see the same principles applied in the Community. The intellectual climate has recently been moving in a more liberal direction, but traditions so deeply embedded in the national character take a long time to alter. As Simon Nora, the head of the Ecole Nationale d'Administration (ENA), the forcing ground for France's top administrators, put it in 1985 when describing his students' reaction to the latest economic ideas: 'They now believe that it is the state's job to teach the country to be more liberal.'[15] Helmut Schmidt has argued that it will take 'three generations to reshape the essential core of the ENA tradition into a belief in free trade'.[16] France distrusts the opening up of markets, the breaking down of barriers and free competition across frontiers, which might lead to French companies losing out to foreigners. It prefers a more organized system whereby French companies trade advantages in their market for openings in another on a reciprocal basis. It also has a strong instinctive preference for planning industrial development through choosing companies to carry the national or European standard, favouring domestic or European suppliers against outsiders and organizing public purchasing for the benefit of companies enjoying official approval.

At any one time, therefore, France has a number of specific projects to push, such as the extension of its high-speed train network into neighbouring countries, or a new initiative in telecommunications, space or some other high-technology field in which French companies are seeking to play a leading role. What it wants is technical help, money or markets from its neighbours. Sometimes it is primarily interested in finding a single partner, in which case Germany or Britain are the most likely; on other occasions it is looking for several. Its attitude as to whether the Community framework or some other arrangement is more appropriate will depend entirely on circumstances. But the approach is constant; if France wants something then it must by definition be European. As President Mitterrand put it, after the 1985 Bonn World Economic Summit, when explaining why other European countries should be more attracted to France's Eureka project than participation in the American Strategic Defence Initiative: 'Europe must mobilize itself around a great project that is truly European.'[17]

Finally, and quite apart from these considerations, the French still harbour fears of Germany derived from the past, in particular that the Federal Republic might somehow be tempted to slip its moorings in the West and slide off into some form of neutralism in search of reunification. The result would no doubt be very different from Bismarck's Second Reich, let alone Hitler's Third. But whatever form it might take, even the thought of a united Germany still causes nightmares in France, as does the vision of a neutralist vacuum between the French frontier and the forward position of the Warsaw Pact armies. The possibility, no matter how remote, that these two spectres might be combined is enough to strike fear into all French breasts. That is why official and intellectual circles in Paris speculate in a manner that others sometimes find obsessive about 'the German Question', the implications of the Greens or the neutralists in the Social Democratic Party, or whatever other political or intellectual current happens to be running strongly in Germany. They have an acute awareness, born of centuries of rivalry, that the security of France depends on stability in Germany and on whether Germany is inclining towards the Western or Eastern aspect of her character and geographical situation.

That is why President Mitterrand, who himself had voted against the 1963 Franco-German Treaty, marked its twentieth anniversary with a speech in the Bundestag in effect urging German MPs to remain loyal to the Atlantic Alliance and to allow the deployment of more American missiles on German soil. It explains too why the French government is always anxious to encourage the Germans to regard European Union as an alternative to purely German national aspirations, or at any rate as a vehicle for fulfilling them, and to respond to whatever efforts their government might make in that direction.

An example of this occurred in 1984 and 1985 when the German people had to contend with a difficult combination of problems. On the one hand relations with East Germany were going through a bad patch, which included the cancellation of the long-awaited visit to Bonn of the East German head of government, Erich Honecker. On the other the wartime allies were engaged in an apparently ceaseless round of celebrations commemorating the Normandy Landings, VE Day and various connected events, which were bound to arouse difficult psychological and emotional problems for the Germans. The Bonn government understandably felt a need to reassure its people that the Federal Republic really was accepted by its partners as a true and reliable friend and ally. Its calls for a new push towards European Union were one of the ways in which it tried to achieve this. The French responses were designed to provide the necessary credibility and so to help anchor the Federal Republic more firmly than ever in the West. They were also backed by imaginative symbolic gestures, which may appear theatrical outside the Franco-German context and cannot be reproduced in others, such as the occasion on which President Mitterrand and Chancellor Kohl held hands on the battlefield of

Verdun, but they make a profound impact on German public opinion.

Germany

The Federal Republic's position in the Community and attitudes towards it are, like so much else in Germany, complex and full of contradictions. 'The Germans,' Goethe once said, 'make everything difficult, both for themselves and for everyone else.' There are many reasons why this should be so in Europe.

At a purely operational level the fact that West Germany is the only federation among all the member states, and that the Bonn government, unlike others, must contend with 'states' rights' in the form of the *Lander*, is a major consideration. Where money is involved this can be extremely important. The government itself is also far less homogeneous than is normally the case with the French or British, with individual departments in Bonn enjoying a degree of autonomy untrammelled by central co-ordination in a way that is unknown in Paris or London. Their internal policy debates are accordingly more exposed and usually more protracted than those of the other two capitals, with the result that it is harder for an outsider to discern what exactly 'the Germans are after'. This is a point that the British – with, by most continental standards, an exceptionally tightly knit and highly co-ordinated government machine – have difficulty in understanding.

At a more profound level lies the legacy of Germany's past. Alone among Western Europeans the nation is divided; and not just in two, but between East and West with profound implications for the national psyche. The sense of guilt for what was done during the Hitler era is still felt and still influences German political attitudes and decisions. At the same time there is resentment against those outside Germany who seek to play on it and to keep alive the memories of that time. There is a sense of justifiable pride in what the Federal Republic has achieved in terms of democracy, stability and, for want of a better term, good citizenship, in the Community and the Western Alliance, coupled with an awareness that anti-Germanism is still a potent, albeit normally hidden, force in other European countries.

This prejudice manifests itself at a personal and political level. During the British budget row when Germany, a larger contributor than the United Kingdom, began to ask for some abatement to be made to its contribution as well, one of my Commission colleagues took me aside at a party to give me his opinion. 'We should help Britain,' he said, 'because it is poor and anyway it is Britain, but not Germany because it is rich and it is Germany.' On another occasion after I had tabled a proposal on behalf of the Commission designed to deal with the British problem and to safeguard the German interest as part of an overall settlement, I sought privately to enlist the support of Dutch and Italian government officials. Their concern and their objections centred overwhelmingly on the fact that Germany stood to gain something, even though German agreement was indispensable to resolving this Community problem; and that, unless something was done, Germany would be the only substantial net payer into the budget without the reassurance of any kind of ceiling being placed on its liability. As those who made these points were quick to point out, the Federal Republic receives enormous non-budgetary benefits from the Community, including a special trading relationship with East Germany, and was itself responsible for many of the absurdities of the Common Agricultural Policy that lay at the root of the British problem. None the less an element of real prejudice, both personal and reflecting the feelings of the electorate of the

countries concerned, came through. Germany is still not regarded as being just another country, like all the rest, and the
Germans know it.

It was above all to tackle this problem that, led by Chancellor
Adenauer, they responded so enthusiastically to the set of post-
war initiatives that resulted in the European Coal and Steel
Community and the European Economic Community, and as-
pired to the European Defence Community backed up by a
political community. They saw in them a means to secure
rehabilitation and respectability as well as being excited by the
challenge of building something out of the ashes of one war that
would prevent others. If the French in some way look on the
Community as a ladder whereby others can become more like
them, it was for Germany the ladder on which they could indeed
become more like others. By joining in the general effort to build
a new European Union they could put behind them all the
particular problems associated with their own nationality and
past.

Adenauer's aim and those of his government were shaped by
three primary considerations. The first was that there should
quite simply never be another war, either with France or on
German soil. The second was that Germany should never revert
to her traditional policy of balancing between East and West, a
policy that itself had been a cause of so much instability in
Europe. He wanted not only the Federal Republic to be irreversi-
bly incorporated into the West, but for there never again to be
any doubt in German or other minds that this was so. The third
consideration was that the Germans of the Federal Republic
should be enabled to live with the fact of a divided nation and
the hope of a reunited one without ever trying to turn that hope
into reality in a way that would once again endanger Europe's
peace and stability.

Monnet's idea of a Community based on a legal framework of unlimited duration and leading to a united Europe provided a vehicle for the attainment of all these objectives. Simultaneously it provided reconciliation with France, and integration into the West. At the same time it established the framework within which the people of a divided nation could dream of a new form of union in the context of a united Europe. General de Gaulle, on his return to power in 1958, saw how much it was in France's interest to encourage and help Adenauer in his historic work. Sadly, the British, blinded by their own distrust of supranational theories, could not.

The idea of a Community leading to European Union is still frequently invoked by Germans as being essential to provide their fellow countrymen with a national purpose and means of fulfilling their aspirations in something other than a purely German context. The cry, part plea part threat, that 'unless the other countries of the Community are prepared to work with us in building a united Europe our people will revert to nationalism' is a familiar theme of German contributions at private and unofficial international gatherings. At the highest political level Chancellor Kohl himself frequently draws a link between the very existence of the Federal Republic and the European ideal. 'We know there can be no returning to Otto von Bismarck's nation state,' he said at Oxford in his Adenauer Memorial Lecture on 2 May 1984. 'Our passionate advocacy of European unification stems to a great extent from awareness that a peaceful settlement of the German question is only conceivable within a greater European framework.' A few months later in January 1985 he told the prestigious international Davos Management Forum that 'Being the driving force behind European unification is one of the Federal Republic's reasons for existence.'[18]

THE REASONS FOR REALITY

In Adenauer's time nationalism was even more discredited in Germany than elsewhere and it was possible for Germans to hope, or at least dream, that the concept of European unity might one day be applied to the whole of Europe, and so to the whole of Germany. All that has changed. Germans have recovered their sense of national identity and national feeling, not necessarily in the same way as other people, but no less strongly. It has also become clear that the division of Europe, and thus of Germany, is permanent for as far ahead as the eye can see.

The Federal Republic has responded to this immensely difficult and complex combination in a manner that would have seemed unthinkable at any previous period of history. It has not sought special German solutions to German problems that would involve weakening its links with the West in an effort to draw East Germany away from the East. It has recognized reality and, as Adenauer hoped, integrated itself as firmly as possible into the West in both the Community and NATO contexts. From that secure base it has sought to promote good relations between East and West and within that framework as close a set of relationships, personal contacts and trading links between the two Germanies as possible. Without calling into question the frontier between the two states it seeks by whatever means it can to ensure that the relationship between them is as 'special' as constant effort and attention can make it. No other Western European country is faced with such a continuously demanding task.

It is not the purpose of this book to analyse the Federal Republic's *Ostpolitik* nor its *Deutschlandpolitik*. What matters here is that the West Germans have chosen to root both firmly in their *Westpolitik*, in other words the Community and NATO. Thus the capacity of those two organizations to inspire their confidence and to provide them with the role, opportunities and advantages they need is crucial. Should the Community and NATO lose that capacity the whole basis on which the Federal Republic has conducted itself since its foundation would be put at risk. The French nightmare of it slipping its moorings in the West might become a reality.

It is against this background that one must see German rhetoric about European Union and the constant efforts by German ministers to generate enthusiasm for the idea. The German predilection for new treaties, so evident in 1984 and 1985, fits naturally into this approach, as well as harking back to Adenauer and his search for irreversible commitments that would bind the Federal Republic to the West and give her a role there.

Among non-Germans, however, the rhetoric can create misunderstandings. With such words as Chancellor Kohl's about the purpose of the Federal Republic ringing in one's ears one might suppose, to paraphrase President Kennedy, that the Federal Republic would be prepared to pay any price and make any sacrifice in the cause of European unity. But one would be wrong. This is one of the points at which the contradictions in the German position become apparent. In European affairs they talk as idealists, expect others to do the same and even judge them to a great extent by their willingness to do so. In the 1950s and 1960s they were up to a point prepared to act as idealists as well, but those days are past.

During the 1970s and even more in the 1980s it became apparent that, regardless of rhetoric, German governments of both parties would judge proposals for new European policies increasingly in terms of straightforward German interests, usually rather narrowly defined. In practice this means two things. Firstly, as the largest contributor to the Community budget they will not support anything that costs money unless they are sure that everything possible has first been done to reduce the size of the bill, or that it directly favours German interests. Secondly, as believers in market forces and confident of their own capacity to compete, they are invariably suspicious of far-reaching and *dirigiste* plans for European policies organized from Brussels.

The fact is that although the idea of European Union continues to exercise a powerful attraction over German minds, the reality of the Community does not. The constant rows of the 1970s and 1980s have been deeply disillusioning. Many in the Federal Republic regard Community policies in relation to steel, textiles, international trade and, above all, agriculture as economically unsound, even when supported by their own government. They also fear that the Federal Republic itself may be contaminated by what they regard as the lax and mistaken economic policies of other countries. It was this anxiety that led to much of the domestic opposition to Schmidt's original initiative over the European Monetary System. He was able to overcome it at the time, but in the years that followed, the suspicions and opposition of the Bundesbank (the central bank) and of business circles ensured that Germany would not help to develop it further. In addition to their distrust of much of what takes place in Europe's name, the Germans feel that insufficient attention is paid to problems that they care about, especially in the environmental field where their concern over such matters as dying forests and pollution of the North Sea is altogether greater than people in other countries generally realize.

Finally there is the question of money. In November 1876, in relation to a quite different set of problems, Bismarck confided the following thought to his diary: 'I have always heard politicians use the word Europe when they were making requests to other powers which they did not dare formulate in the name of their own country.'[19] German public opinion today tends very often to regard the European proposals of other countries and of the Commission in this light; in other words as devices to squeeze money out of German pockets to finance activities of which Germans would not approve in their own country, let alone elsewhere.

The result of this disillusionment, through an amalgam of emotional and practical considerations not all of which are consistent with each other, is to bind Germany more closely than ever to France. Within the general idea of European Union lies the particular concept of reconciliation between previously warring peoples, with Germany, through the Community, playing its full part in European and international affairs. That continues to exercise a strong hold and for historical reasons is taken to refer above all to France. The set of European initiatives taken by France in the 1950s and the 1963 Treaty of Friendship between the two countries have always been regarded as the major achievement of the European idea. The more unsatisfactory the practical aspects of the Community, the more important it becomes to sustain and nurture it.

In practical terms this means that a German leader gains marks with his electorate if he can show that he is 'well in' with the French, while to be on bad terms with them is to court unpopularity and distrust. To be received in Paris, and even better in the French President's private residence, with the same warmth as his predecessor is a matter of real political significance to an incoming German Chancellor. If the subsequent rhythm of his meetings with the French President were to indicate that the two countries were drifting apart he would be put on the defensive at the bar of public opinion. This is a card that French leaders play with considerable skill.

Moreover, heads of state and government hate meeting without having something to show for it. Consequently, the frequency of Franco-German Summits on the one hand coupled with the attitude of German public opinion on the other combine to bring forward a variety of Franco-German initiatives that might not otherwise see the light of day. Sometimes they remain purely Franco-German; on other occasions they are put into a Community context. Either way the frequency of the Summits serves to reinforce the two countries' leadership role.

Although French and German policy assumptions and objectives often differ, the knowledge that when they do agree they can usually get what they want and, at the very least, prevent anyone else from doing what they don't want is a powerful link. With the brutality that characterizes one side of his nature, Helmut Schmidt has expressed it in these terms: 'Italy is notorious for its lack of government. Britain is notorious for governments, Labour or Conservative, that think the Atlantic is narrower than the Channel. That leaves only the French and Germans. So it is up to the Elysée Palace in Paris and the Federal Chancellery in Bonn.'[20]

In the interview from which this quotation is taken Schmidt sets out some ideas whereby France and Germany together could dramatically reduce Germany's dependence on the United States for its defence. France would extend the scope of its *force de frappe* to German territory, and the two countries would strengthen their conventional forces so that together these 'would be a deterrent to the Russians'. Few Germans, however, would be prepared to put their faith in such an arrangement. They believe that the only way a threat by one superpower can be deterred is by the strength of the other, and that the Federal Republic's security is thus ultimately dependent on the United States.

Whatever may be said, therefore, about Britain's view of

the Channel and the Atlantic, there are few things German governments dislike more than having to make a similar choice. They will go to great lengths to prevent a situation from arising in which they are faced with a choice between their American protectors and their French partners. But sometimes it happens, as in 1985 when President Reagan invited Europeans to participate in the research phase of the Strategic Defence Initiative while President Mitterrand presented the French Eureka project as a rival and as a litmus test of France's Community partners' European good intentions. The embarrassment of the German government was plain for all to see. Such events, though, are likely to remain rare, since Bonn, Paris and Washington all know that France and the United States are both essential to anchoring the Federal Republic firmly in the West, and that if German attitudes towards the two countries should ever go through a bad patch at the same time those in the Federal Republic who wish to call that attachment into question would be greatly strengthened.

Italy

Despite Schmidt's dismissive references to Italy's lack of government, Italian attitudes towards Europe in general and the Community in particular have been more consistent than those of other major powers. From the outset Italians have been inspired by the vision of a united Europe and the grand designs for achieving it. To them it has always seemed a noble concept, recalling their own long struggle for national unification and a natural continuation of it. The idea of unity as such – as distinct from Europe as a field for fulfilling national ambitions and promoting national interests – has from the very beginning aroused genuine enthusiasm in Italy and continues to do so now.

To some extent, it must be said, this results from the deep dissatisfaction that Italians have felt, ever since their own unification was achieved, with their own domestic politics. The Risorgimento, coming as it did after centuries of foreign occupation and disunity, was accompanied by and carried along on a tidal wave of rhetoric and expectations. It was expected, if not at one bound then over time, to eradicate the evil consequences of Italy's previous condition and transform the country into a modern state comparable with Britain or France. United Italy, however, turned out to be a massive disappointment: 'A rickety, divided, shabby, impoverished and backward nation, yet one that wasted its miserable resources trying to impersonate the great powers', in the damning words of the Italian writer Luigi Barzini.[21] For a while Mussolini captured the national imagination, but in the end he left the country defeated, humiliated and ashamed. In the post-war years the dream of a United Europe took the place in Italian minds held for many centuries by the dream of a United Italy as the great hope for the future that would bring good government and modernization in its train.

Since then Italy has achieved a great deal in social, economic and industrial terms and, notwithstanding its constant changes of government, a considerable degree of underlying political stability and continuity of policy as well. A foreigner can appreciate that. But the constant scandals, corruption and conspiracies of party politics, the patronage and inefficiency of so much of the state sector, the continuing problems of organized crime and political violence make it impossible for Italians to admire or even respect their own national public life.

Europe remains the great hope for the future. It also provides a sort of political equivalent to emigrating and seeking a new life and opportunities elsewhere. Whatever may be happening at home, Italian politicians can play a prominent and constructive role on the Community stage trying to make the institutions work and seeking solutions to the problems of others. They are unusually dedicated in their approach to these tasks and often very effective. Their goodwill is legendary. Public opinion takes pride in their activities and when an Italian government secures a European success, even one that does not directly promote the national interest, it can expect to receive plaudits at home.

The Italian achievement, while holding the Community presidency in the first half of 1985, in bringing the enlargement negotiations with Spain and Portugal to a successful conclusion after eight years provides a spectacular but not untypical example of their abilities. At one stage their Foreign Minister, Giulio Andreotti, in a record-breaking marathon, chaired forty hours of talks without a break for sleep. He was heard to remark: 'After twenty-five years in Italian government it's really not so difficult.'[22] The previous record of thirty-four hours was held by a budget negotiation in which I had participated and, despite my experience of the long hours of the House of Commons, I found it very difficult indeed.

Not only have Italians felt dissatisfied with their internal situation since unification, they have also struggled continuously to be treated as a great power on a par with France, Britain and Germany. The Community, with its rules and procedures, provides a means of helping them to achieve that goal. The French and Germans are primarily interested in each other and in the opportunities that co-operation between them can create. They consider themselves, both instinctively and on the basis of experience, to be Europe's central focus and its natural leaders. The British, when they are not cutting themselves off from everyone else, equally instinctively think in terms of inter-state relationships and of trying to convert the Paris–Bonn axis into a triangle. The Italians, by contrast, are usually hostile to all ideas for a 'directorate' or any other distinction between large and small powers for fear of finding themselves placed in the wrong category. For this reason Italy is both a stronger upholder of conventional Community procedures than the other large countries and invariably anxious not to be left out of anything.

When the European Monetary System was being put together in the latter months of 1978 the government's specialist advisers were doubtful that it would be in Italy's interest to join the exchange rate mechanism if Britain remained out, and had a long list of requirements to be met. Britain did not come in and most of Italy's requirements were not met but Andreotti, at that time Prime Minister, brought the country in none the less. The issue had become, as the Italian press put it, a *test europeo* and thus also a test of Italy's faith in the European ideal and of its capacity to keep up with the Joneses in the shape of France and Germany. For the British the word 'isolation' in the context of Europe calls to mind the adjective 'splendid'; for the Italians it would be the opposite.

There is a strong feeling in Italy that a number of Community policies have not treated the country fairly. The Common Agricultural Policy is thought, with some reason, to have operated in a fashion that favours northern products as against those from the Mediterranean. The common external trade policy is subjected to similar accusations of bias, and so, for a long time, was the steel policy. Although others tend to find the Italians wily and capable negotiators, able to defend their national interest as well as anyone, they themselves constantly complain of being hard done by. There is an element of pretence about this; the more one can claim and, if possible, show that one is making more sacrifices for the common good than others, the more one can press for better terms next time or on some other issue. Nevertheless, the grievance is also genuinely felt, and Italian public opinion is prone to believe that the country's interests do not receive the same consideration as those of other large countries.

This does not, however, shake the national faith in the Community; almost the contrary. Because Italians feel that their bureaucracy, economy and social structures are inefficient and old fashioned by comparison with those of their northern neighbours, they see the Community as an essential means of keeping in touch with the mainstream of European progress and development. Without it, they fear, they would be in danger of slipping off into some Mediterranean frontier land between the first and third worlds. Hard, therefore, as Italians may find Community rules and disciplines, they regard them as essential to enable Italy to remain on equal terms with those countries in Europe with which they would wish to be compared. They also understand that those rules and disciplines bring tangible gains by providing far greater opportunities than the domestic market alone would be able to offer to those sectors of the Italian economy, and they are numerous, that are as good as or better than the rest of Europe.

Besides, these rules can be taken with a pinch of salt. By contrast with its record as one of the best Community citizens in terms of trying to make the institutions work and to resolve problems, Italy is one of the worst when it comes to observing the rules that have been established. Whenever the Commission draws up lists of the cases it is conducting against the various member states, Italy is invariably one of the main offenders (see Table 4, p. 89). In this respect Italian behaviour in the Community reflects the behaviour of individual Italians towards laws and the payment of taxes within their own country; just as the one is regarded by the individuals concerned as in no way derogating from their national loyalty, so the other is considered to be perfectly compatible with loyalty to the Community. Citizens of more strait-laced countries may find this hard to accept, but it is so.

The Smaller Countries

It is as difficult to generalize about the smaller member countries as about the larger. Each has its own distinctive personality and the differences between them are immense. All, however, have one thing in common. They benefit substantially from the very existence of the Community.

Their trade, as Table 2 on p. 40 shows, is overwhelmingly dependent on it and thus their industry and agriculture. They are all net beneficiaries from the budget and some substantially so. The Community's rules and procedures provide them with a capacity to influence the policies of their larger partners that would once have seemed impossible. Just as British Prime Ministers delight in being received in Washington, so those of the smaller countries enjoy attending European Councils on equal terms with the French President, British Prime Minister and German Chancellor. When a small country holds the six-monthly rotating presidency its head of government has the added pleasure of being able to invite these and other notables to meetings in his own country and to present his government to the electors as the arbiter of Europe's affairs. Nobody who has had to sacrifice weekends travelling to and from ministerial gatherings in the west of Ireland or on Greek islands that could just as well have been held in more accessible locations, and has seen the attention they receive from the host country's media, could underestimate the political advantages some small countries' governments believe stem from these activities. The presidency also provides such governments' ministers with the chance, albeit fleetingly, to speak on behalf of the whole Community at international gatherings and conferences. Through the institution of Political Co-operation they are brought into touch with diplomatic affairs in other parts of the world that would normally pass them by.

The Community's language rules put Dutch, Danish and Greek on an equal footing with English and French; even if it does not work out quite like that in practice, this is something they are not even theoretically accorded anywhere else and that they value greatly. So greatly in fact that ministers and officials from those countries who speak excellent English, French or German will insist on conducting business in their own language in the Council of Ministers, regardless of the cost and complication involved in providing simultaneous interpretation. The Community's institutions provide opportunities for the nationals of the smaller countries to pursue careers beyond their own frontiers, which are also highly prized even, at the highest political levels, as the decision of a former Danish Prime Minister, Jens Otto Krag, to become the Commission's representative in Washington, and of a former Dutch deputy Foreign Minister, Laurens-Jan Brinkhorst, to take on the same job in Tokyo, shows. The list, in short, is extensive and varied.

For some small countries the Community confers additional special advantages. For Ireland, for instance, joining provided a historic opportunity to reduce its economic dependence on the United Kingdom and to find an international stage on which to operate as well as bringing huge financial benefits, estimated at 6 per cent of its gross domestic product in 1982.[23] For Belgians it provides an escape route from the sterile division between

Flemish and Walloons that dominates life within their own country, and a chance to find a role beyond it within which both can work together. The vast numbers of Belgians who flock to work for the Community institutions provide an indication of how much they value this. Belgium and Luxembourg also gain from the physical presence of the Community's institutions on their territory and the revenue, employment and international attention that this generates.

Besides gaining enormously from their membership, the small countries, not surprisingly, tend to be very suspicious of the larger ones so far as the Community's management and rules are concerned. Like Italy, they abhor the idea of a two- or three-power 'directorate' emerging and strongly support the official institutions, the powers and influence of which they wish to see enhanced. At times their unease about big power collaboration and influence can reach such a pitch that during the final stages of the British budget problem I sometimes had the impression that they would almost rather see it continue than be settled in such a way as to bring the big three closer together.

Because of their strong support for the institutions and Community rules the small countries are often regarded, and regard themselves, as specially 'good Europeans' as distinct from the more selfish and nationalistic larger countries. In fact, they can be just as determined to uphold their own narrow national interests as their larger partners. One example of this is the way the Luxembourg government argues – right up to the level of Foreign Ministers' meetings – for the maintenance of particular Commission activities in the Grand Duchy, sometimes involving only a handful of officials, and its action in the European Court against the European Parliament for ceasing to meet there. The long Irish rearguard action against the introduction of controls on surplus milk production is another. Although some of the richer small countries, like Holland and Denmark, have for long been substantial beneficiaries from the Community budget, they were for years deeply resistant to giving up anything to reduce the British burden. In essence the main difference between large and small countries, so far as the defence of national interests is concerned, is that the small have fewer irons in the fire and lack the power to defend them for so long.

Between the small countries themselves, however, there is one crucial difference. The Benelux trio – Belgium, Holland and Luxembourg – were among the original Six and continue to regard themselves as core members of the Community, and of all other forms of European activity. They all want to see closer European integration and are still much attracted, like Italy, to the supranational ideal. Also like Italy, they would invariably wish to be part of whatever schemes the French and Germans might be hatching. This would even apply if a particular scheme seemed contrary to their national interest, since they know that in the last resort they cannot stop those countries once they have decided on something, and would consider that their own interests can more easily be defended from within than without. In any circumstances they would hate to see France and Germany going ahead without them, and would regard that in itself as being contrary to their deepest interest. In other words, they view their involvement in what is happening in Europe in dynamic rather than static terms.

There is one major proviso to this. Rich though they are and notwithstanding their gains from the Community budget in its present form, they do not like spending money on other people. Contrary to what their public pronouncements about developing the Community might lead one to expect, my experience over eight years in the Budget Council is that they wish to keep transfers to the poorer countries through such Community spending policies as the regional and social funds to the minimum they can get away with. It was very rare for them to support the additions suggested by the European Parliament or by the poorer countries themselves.

Denmark is even more tight-fisted than the Benelux countries and, on top of that, at the opposite end of the spectrum when it comes to considering other forms of involvement. It joined the Community only because, once Britain did, both its major trading partners – Germany being the other – would be members and it could not afford to stay out. Its approach has always been utterly self-interested and it invariably adopts a minimalist view of everything to do with Europe and the Community. Its attitude was aptly described to me by a Danish MEP in these terms: 'Scandinavia is the mistress whom we love. The Community is the rich wife who keeps us.' Ireland has some Danish characteristics, but as a major beneficiary of Community spending programmes is much in favour of their expansion. It is normally inclined to join whatever is afoot, both because that policy has paid in the past (in literal terms) and in order still further to weaken the link with Britain. Like Denmark, though, it is deeply reluctant to become involved in anything touching on defence and security, which in turn is likely to affect the two countries' approach to foreign policy co-operation.

The Newcomers

For the three newest members, Greece, Spain – which is midway between the large and the small, and classified with the large – and Portugal, the Community represents both a recognition that they are part of the mainstream of Western European development and a means to secure that position. Not for them the federalist ideals of an earlier age; their concerns are more immediate, down-to-earth and, in a perfectly honourable sense, self-centred. 'What does Portugal want from the Common Market?' *Le Figaro* asked António Marta, president of the governmental committee for integration into the Community, in May 1984. 'It should consolidate our democracy,' he replied, 'and it will be the motor of its modernization.'[24] On the day the enlargement negotiations finally ended in March 1985 the Portuguese Prime Minister, Mário Soares, expressed the same thought in more ecstatic terms. 'I think everything will change,' he said. 'In five years Portugal will be a different country.'[25] Portugal is more backward than Spain and behind Greece as well, but those are among the reasons why they too sought membership.

Greece under Andreas Papandreou has not been an easy partner. On the one hand it wants to maximize its material gains, while on the other it is always on the look-out for ways of impressing its own public opinion by cocking a snook at its partners. Its level of economic and bureaucratic development is also such that even with goodwill, which has often been lacking, it would be very difficult indeed for its economy and society to adapt to some of the Community's rules and regulations. Portugal, which seems likely to prove a more co-operative partner, will face some of the same problems. Spain is an altogether different matter being much more advanced than the other two in both economic and bureaucratic terms as well as much larger. Its history, however, does not suggest that it will find it easy to adjust to the constant search for compromise that characterizes Community affairs. Like Britain it enters the Community with a national character forged by history into a very different mould from that of many of its new partners.

Britain

Which brings us to Britain, the country that has been at the centre of more Community rows than any other. Immediately on entering the Foreign and Commonwealth Office through the ambassadors' entrance, just behind the Mountbatten statue on Horse Guards Parade, one is confronted by a picture of the Tower of Babel by Christian Micker. It is badly lit and needs a clean so that one has to look closely before realizing what it is. Often when passing it on my way to the Foreign Secretary's room above it seemed to provide an appropriate symbol for the misunderstandings that had dogged Britain's relationship with the Community since refusing to become involved with the original Schuman Plan in 1950 and since joining on 1 January 1973.

The extent of the problem was well put by Tony Crosland when, as Foreign Secretary, he addressed the European Parliament at the outset of the first British presidency of the Council of Ministers in January 1977. The Community, he said, represented Britain's first permanent peacetime engagement on the continent of Europe since the Reformation. Since that time Britain has, of course, participated in many alliances and fought in many wars. It always sought to prevent a single power or combination of powers from acquiring a dominant position and strived to maintain open markets. But from the reign of Queen Elizabeth I until the post-war period Britain's eyes and interests were directed more towards the wider world. The emotional commitments of the British people followed suit. Unlike the French and Dutch, who also had great overseas empires, they did not really feel part of mainland Europe. In that respect their experience has something in common with the Spanish. As a result the British failed in the 1950s to appreciate that, if they remained out of the efforts being made to form a European

Community, they would simultaneously open the way for a combination of powers to dominate the Continent politically and economically and cut themselves off from what, in the second half of the twentieth century, would be their own principal sphere of political and economic interest.

The Community thus became the only international organization of which Britain is now a member of which it was not a founder member. In all the others it was 'present at the creation' (to borrow the title of Dean Acheson's memoirs), helped to lay the foundations and has been part of all the subsequent evolutionary stages. In some cases – NATO and the Commonwealth perhaps – this is a source of pride; in others, notably permanent membership of the United Nations Security Council, it is a continuing source of privilege. In the Community Britain arrived late, thanks to her own aloofness at the outset followed by de Gaulle's veto in 1963. The mould had been set and even in the most favourable circumstances the subsequent adjustment process would have been difficult. The medieval king Alfonso the Wise of Castile is credited with saying, 'Had I been present at the creation, I would have given some useful hints for the better ordering of the universe.' It is not surprising that the British when confronted by certain aspects of the Community should feel the same way.

As it was, the circumstances were far from favourable. The Treaty of Rome was signed just as the long post-war boom was moving into overdrive, and the first stage of the Community's development coincided with the optimism and burgeoning prosperity of the 1960s. British accession, by contrast, came just as that boom was about to end with the first oil shock, and its first years of membership coincided with the worst recession since the 1930s.

The psychological and political background was as unfavourable as the economic. The vast majority of British people and their leaders were completely untouched by the wave of idealism on which the Community had originally been launched. Far from finding federalism and supranationalism inspiring ideals the British viewed them with the gravest suspicion. The same applied to the Community's institutions. Nor did the concept of reconciliation that had such a profound impact in France and Germany carry the same weight in Britain. For one thing by 1963, and even more by 1973, the wartime memories of the Community's formative years were fading; for another the British had in any case never felt the same deep and hereditary hostility towards their enemies as had the French and Germans.

They were, as a result, badly placed to appreciate the full significance of the Franco-German reconciliation and the aims of the two countries. Perhaps if they had, Britain could have played the role of 'godparent' in the reconciliation process, or at least gained some credit for helping it along, and so come to be regarded as an indispensable element in the key relationship that lies at the heart of Europe. In the event it was formed with Britain on the sidelines – initially sceptical of what was being attempted, later unconcerned at not being involved, and in the last few years increasingly worried about being excluded and trying to break in.

For the most part the British entered the Community in an unemotional frame of mind. There were some enthusiasts, but the majority of those in favour of entry were ruled by their heads rather than their hearts. They had discovered, in the phrase immortalized by Lord Stockton when he was Prime Minister, that they could no longer command 'a place at the top table', that the Commonwealth did not provide the power and influence that had been expected, that no alternative European grouping was viable and that the continued success of the Community posed a threat to the British economy. In a nutshell Britain was turning away from a set of assumptions and policies that had failed, towards an experiment that seemed to be succeeding, in the hope that it would yield political influence and economic growth that could not be obtained by other means. Even the turn itself was a difficult and controversial manoeuvre opposed by a significant minority in the country at large and by most of the Labour Party whenever it was in opposition. Neither Parliament's vote approving the accession arrangements nor the large majority in favour of staying in at the 1975 referendum resolved the matter. British membership remained controversial and withdrawal a real possibility until the general election of 1983.

From the outset things went wrong. For purely domestic reasons the incoming Labour government in 1974 launched what was called a 're-negotiation' of the original entry terms. Such an initiative so soon after joining was bound to use up goodwill and cause irritation, even though it changed nothing of substance. Its real damage, however, came later. In 1975, at the conclusion of the re-negotiation, Harold Wilson, as Prime Minister, and James Callaghan, as Foreign Secretary, said that all Britain's problems, including those connected with the Community budget, had been resolved. Yet in 1978 Callaghan, who had by then himself become Prime Minister, was again demanding changes on the grounds that otherwise Britain would shortly become the largest net contributor to the Community budget.

This time the British were right, as most governments' private calculations must have shown, and as a Commission report the following year was to confirm.[26] But the reluctance of others to accept the British case was understandable. The ink on the re-negotiation arrangements was hardly dry. Moreover, Britain under Labour had been a conspicuously difficult and unhelpful partner over a whole range of Community activities, and two of the government's most prominent members, John Silkin and Tony Benn, had continued their anti-EEC campaign while participating in the work of the Council of Ministers; something many on the Continent found shocking. Nor had the British government even made any serious attempt to reduce its prospective deficit by supporting the development of Community policies, such as energy, that would have been to its financial advantage. Not surprisingly the other member states were fed up with Britain – in addition, of course, to benefiting from the arrangements about which the British were complaining.

Then came the June 1979 Conservative election victory and a marvellous opportunity to put the relationship between Britain and the rest of the Community on to a new footing to the benefit of all concerned. As 'the party of Europe', which had taken Britain in, led the fight to keep it there during the referendum and, during Labour's years in office, argued for a more constructive and wholehearted commitment, the Conservatives wanted 'to make Europe work'. It was in the interest of the incoming government to make a new start and to establish better relations with its partners. The problem was the budget and the fear of becoming a net contributor to the tune of nearly £1 billion a year from 1980 onwards. It barred the way to a new start like a fall of rock on a mountain road.

It was at this point that an act of statesmanship was required and notably from Chancellor Schmidt and President Giscard d'Estaing. They were not simply the leaders of the two most powerful countries in the Community. They were the doyens of the European Council, close personal friends and close allies. They were the men on whom at that time everything in Europe depended. Together they could certainly have solved the British budget problem before it got out of hand. What they should have done was to take Mrs Thatcher aside, show understanding for what was after all a genuine problem for which her government was in no way responsible and offer an 'out of court' settlement. The Commission paper referred to above, analysing the problem and quantifying the likely British deficit, which the European Council had asked for in June and which was published in September, provided an ideal basis for a quiet, behind-the-scenes negotiation and agreement.

Instead, as the November 1979 European Council approached, it became apparent that the French and German leaders had decided to embark on a trial of strength with their new British colleague. Mrs Thatcher would be isolated and alone and, it was thought, unable to withstand a combined onslaught from all the rest. 'This meeting will show what your Prime Minister is made of,' a senior French official said to me with relish as he prepared to set off for Dublin Castle, where the Council was to be held. And so it did.

Schmidt and Giscard d'Estaing promoted a derisory offer and every pressure was brought to bear on Mrs Thatcher to accept. She responded by demanding 'my money back', a phrase that was widely regarded as an attack on the whole principle on which the Community's 'own resources' system of financing is based. As the vehemence of her arguments increased, Schmidt at one point feigned sleep, and when she refused to give in the French party's cars were drawn up outside with their engines revving in order to emphasize the take-it-or-leave-it nature of what was on offer. Finally the meeting ended in deadlock. Already dubbed the Iron Lady by Moscow, Dublin enshrined Mrs Thatcher as 'la Dame de Fer de l'Europe'. From that moment on, in addition to its technical complexities, the British budget problem became inextricably caught up with the pride, prejudices and personalities of the heads of state and government concerned.

Schmidt and Giscard d'Estaing were treating the European Council as a private fief. Their countries were more powerful than any other, and because of the endemic parliamentary instability in most of the rest at that time very few other leaders ever attended more than two or three consecutive meetings. In those circumstances the new British Prime Minister, with enough parliamentary backing to last at least four years, posed a problem. On the one hand she could not be grouped with the transitory leaders of the smaller countries. On the other the big two did not want to become three, both for personal reasons and because of their disenchantment with Britain's record in the Community, as well as doubts about its economic capacity and strength of political purpose. They were 'very patronizing, even rude, in their treatment of her', one of my colleagues in the Commission subsequently told an American journalist. 'They made it clear that she, a mere woman, wouldn't be able to stand up to these two experienced and knowledgeable men in hard negotiation.'[27]

That Mrs Thatcher's sex was a complicating factor I have no doubt. In May 1980 some of the china broken in Dublin was glued back together in the form of an interim settlement, regarded in most capitals as something of a British victory. A few days afterwards a German minister I knew well came to see me. 'You must tell your Prime Minister,' he said, 'that she has hurt my Chancellor in his male pride. If things are to be put right between our two countries, she must find a way of making it up to him.'

The British budget problem became a ball and chain round the Community's ankle. From Dublin in November 1979 until its final solution at Fontainebleau in June 1984 it featured prominently at practically every meeting of the European Council. The interim solutions of May 1980 and June 1982, instead of facilitating the search for a definitive agreement, spawned new sub-problems of their own. It could not be solved at the level of Foreign Ministers because the heads of state and government were personally engaged, and it could not for a long time be solved at their level because the personal prestige of each of the big three was bound up with it, which in turn hardened the resolve of others not to compromise. Even when Schmidt and Giscard d'Estaing had departed from the scene this difficulty remained, as their successors did not want to be accused at home of 'giving way to Mrs Thatcher'. She, for her part, remained implacable.

The consequences of this prolonged failure were far reaching. The longer it lasted the more isolated Britain became and the more this single issue came to dominate British European policy. At times in London and in other capitals it seemed that the British government cared for little else. Such single-mindedness was a mistake. Britain should have tried to break out of the ghetto inherent in any one-against-the-rest situation by going out of its way to demonstrate its commitment to the Community and its desire to see European co-operation carried forward. It should have launched initiatives of its own unconnected with the budget and responded to those of others in a manner designed to attract sympathy and understanding. Instead it concentrated on winning on the narrow budget front and subordinated everything else to that.

Another error was for some time to give the impression of being opposed to the Common Agricultural Policy as such, instead of trying to reform it. As was pointed out in the previous chapter the surpluses that this policy generates and the cost of running it have damaged the Community's reputation in many countries. None the less, along with the Common Market, it remains one of the foundation stones on which the Community is built and an essential element in the basic Franco-German bargain. As such it enjoys a degree of support on the Continent that is incomprehensible in Britain. To call for its modernization and improvement, as many now do – and often in terms that owe much to the original British complaints – is one thing. To give the impression of outright opposition is another. For as long as Britain did so it was bound to provoke the hostility not only of those in all countries who gained from the policy, but also of those who feared that the recurring British demands for changes in the original terms of entry would destroy the delicate balance of the whole Community structure.

In view of the way the rules of the game were set up by Schmidt and Giscard d'Estaing, Mrs Thatcher had no alternative but to be very tough. On the narrow front of the point at issue she was successful. No other European leader could have held out for so long nor secured so much against the opposition of all the rest. The final settlement, in which Britain received a guarantee of a 66 per-cent rebate for future years, was generally considered in most countries to be her victory, and so it was in terms of the distance the two sides had moved from their original positions when the struggle began. But the British failure to combine toughness on the budget with a more constructive and far-sighted approach on other matters meant that the price paid in terms of isolation and lost goodwill was very high. The reputation of the British in many parts of Europe as having no interest in the Community as such and being solely concerned with their own interests, even to the point of putting the Community itself in jeopardy, was confirmed. As a result a further delay, after de Gaulle's veto and the mistakes of the Labour government, was imposed on starting the vital work of establishing Britain alongside France and Germany as one of the principal determinants of European affairs.

The consequences were demonstrated a year later in June 1985, when the British approached the Milan European Council in the confident expectation that their plan for improving decision-making procedures and for a new agreement on Political Co-operation would hold the centre stage. They wanted to be seen at last to be a major influence in Community affairs and to score a negotiating triumph. With the memory of the budget dispute and its outcome still rankling in their minds others were determined to prevent such an outcome. Less than forty-eight hours before the Council convened London was informed that the French and Germans had hijacked the British plan, converting it into a proposal of their own; while at the meeting itself the Italian Prime Minister, Bettino Craxi, used his position in the chair to call a vote on a proposal for an inter-governmental conference, which Mrs Thatcher was known to dislike, in such a way as to force her into a minority of three with the Danes and Greeks. Instead of the diplomatic success for which Mrs Thatcher had hoped, she returned home looking isolated and rebuffed.

Meanwhile British public opinion, never very enthusiastic about the Community, found the budget dispute, after an initial flurry of jingoistic fervour, disillusioning and impossible to understand. Despite this it came to accept the necessity for continued membership because of the strength of the economic arguments, notably those relating to trade and investment, and because of a growing appreciation of the wider political considerations. The lack of any viable alternative also played a part. Against such a background it was impossible to generate any real feeling of commitment comparable to that found, in a variety of different forms, in other countries, and the sense of distance from 'Europe' felt by the British people was reinforced.

This in turn means, now that the budget dispute is settled, that when a British government tries to take an initiative in European affairs it does not receive the same kudos from its electorate as, say, a French or Italian government. The incentive to make the effort is therefore less.

The dispute also forced other governments to look into their own souls and to decide what sort of Community they in practice wished to see. For many of the individuals concerned this was a painful experience, which further heightened their resentment against the British for not putting up and shutting up. When, in the light of the Commission's analysis, they were forced to accept the existence of a British problem the conventional wisdom was that it should be regarded as a temporary aberration. According to this theory it had arisen because the development of the Common Agricultural Policy had not been matched by a similar development of Community spending in other fields. Once the regional and social funds had been built up, and the policies for energy, industry and so on properly launched, the flow of funds out of Britain to finance the CAP would in due course be matched by an inward flow from these activities. *Ergo*, the British problem would disappear, and they should therefore be content with only a modest temporary rebate to bridge the gap between the present problem and the future promise.

This diagnosis and recommended treatment rested on the assumption that the other member states would be prepared to finance the balanced array of other spending policies that had once been envisaged for the Community. Nothing in the behaviour of the richer states over several years suggested that they would. But the dream had continued to coexist with the reality. The need to find a solution to the British problem brought the matter to a head. In order to counter British demands for a large permanent rebate, the other member states were forced to try to agree on new spending policies. In view of their attitudes towards public expenditure, the transfer of wealth from one country to another, and their dissatisfaction with the way existing policies were working, the attempt was bound to fail. But no one likes having to face up to the end of a dream, and because it was the British problem that had brought this particular one to an end an additional twist was given to the already widespread resentment felt towards them. The extent to which the dream of a balanced array of spending policies was abandoned was revealed by the decision on the future financing of the Community, which accompanied the British settlement and which was described in the preceding chapter. It demonstrated beyond doubt that the idea of the Community developing on the basis of common policies commonly financed had been abandoned, at least for some years to come, and that a new direction would have to be charted.

The heads of state and government entered the Château de Fontainebleau, for the meeting at which these decisions were taken, by the Cour des Adieux where Napoleon made his formal farewells before departing for Elba. It was appropriate that they should. By their decisions they were bidding a final farewell to one sort of Community and opening the way to another. The summer weather was better than when the flags in Brussels were flying at half-mast for Hallstein, but the message was the same.

3

Towards a Better Way

Where would the road they had opened up lead? As the heads
of state and government and their retinues left the Château de
Fontainebleau for the last time the mood in the Community was
very mixed. There was relief that at last the British budget
problem had been solved and that both the principle and the
extent of the Community's future financing had been agreed
upon. Earlier in the year the decision had been taken to impose
quotas on milk production, which was widely regarded as the
start of a new and sustained effort to control agricultural costs
and surpluses. So of the major issues that had been dominating
the Community agenda in recent years only the Spanish and
Portuguese enlargement negotiations remained, and the Fontainebleau decisions opened the way for them to be concluded as
well.

The big three all felt pleased with the outcome. Among the
French there was gratification that important decisions had
been taken, and that President Mitterrand had, as they had
hoped at the outset of their presidency six months earlier,
emerged as the arbiter of Europe. The Germans were thankful
that the increase in the Community's financial 'own resources'
had been kept so small, and that some account had been taken

of their complaints about their contribution as well. The British had the most to rejoice about of all. At last after almost six years their budget problem had been disposed of, and they could escape from the ghetto of isolation in which it had imprisoned them.

But there was bitterness as well. Some of the small countries and some in the Commission felt that the extent to which President Mitterrand had wrapped matters up beforehand and behind the scenes with Chancellor Kohl and Mrs Thatcher, and then faced the rest with what amounted to a *fait accompli*, was a dangerous augury. In those governments whose countries gain most from Community expenditure programmes, and among those in the Commission and the European Parliament – of whom there are many – who tend to judge the advance of the European ideal primarily by the rate at which the Community budget expands, there was also disappointment.

Finally there was worry. The British budget problem had become to the Community what a familiar, serious but endurable ailment can be to an individual; that is to say, a permanent excuse for not having to embark on new and hazardous enterprises and a permanent justification for an unsatisfactory way of life. For as long as the problem lasted Britain could be blamed for whatever was wrong in the Community, and the budget issue invoked as a reason why progress could not be expected on other fronts and why no major new initiatives had been undertaken since the launching of the European Monetary System. A German official expressed concern to me about whether his government would now be able to come up with specific proposals to match the expectations inspired by Chancellor Kohl's high-flown rhetoric. A Dane wondered how his government would be able to maintain the opposition to almost any new initiative demanded by its public opinion without becoming a universal object of scorn now that the British were losing their scapegoat role. Like the individual who is told, after many years of being an invalid, that he should begin again to lead a normal life, the Community collectively knew that it should be pleased about the new opportunities that were opening up but in fact felt a good deal of trepidation.

Whenever governments do not know what to do they ask for a report, set up a committee or do both. This is, perhaps, even more true of the Community than it is of national life. In December 1974, when the recession brought on by the first oil shock was beginning to bite and the hopes that had been raised by the first enlargement were being abandoned, Leo Tindemans, who was then Prime Minister of Belgium, was asked to produce a report. Four years later a committee of three, inevitably dubbed the Three Wise Men, was given the task. In 1980 the Commission was given a 'mandate', and at Fontainebleau it was decided to set up two new committees on Institutional Affairs and a People's Europe. The scope, range and objectives of these reports vary, but there is a considerable overlap between them. Taken together they represent a constantly repeated attempt to give the Community a sense of purpose and objectives towards which to work.

That, ever since the end of the federalist dream, has been the Community's fundamental problem. On the one hand it is clear that notwithstanding rhetoric to the contrary it is not in the process of becoming a United States of Europe. On the other it is equally clear that the member states feel themselves bound together by a complex web of shared and common interests. They know they must find a way to organize these interests and the problems and decisions to which they give rise in an orderly and constructive fashion. But they do not know how to do it, nor what sort of institutional, or constitutional, framework would be appropriate. It is not surprising. Nothing remotely like the Community has ever been attempted before, and the Community's membership itself has been constantly changing or about to change for as long as anyone engaged in trying to manage its affairs can remember.

As a constitutional monarch, rather than an executive head of government, Queen Beatrix of Holland was not present at the Fontainebleau deliberations. But a few months earlier she had been invited to address the European Parliament and her speech contained a more perceptive analysis of how to approach Europe's dilemma than some of those produced by the men and women who attend the European Council. 'There are many misconceptions about the unity of Europe,' she said:

For too long people have regarded the growth of the European Community as a development comparable to the evolution of a nation state. In the case of the Community, however, it is not a question of the total transfer of national sovereignty to a new state embracing everyone and everything, but rather the striking of a balance between national and Community powers.[1]

Therein lies the heart of the problem. Governments must find a way of deciding what should be done at the European level and what at the national level. They must also find a better way of administering and executing European policies when they are set up. Political, social and economic priorities will alter with time, and a balance between the national and the European that suits one generation and set of circumstances may well have to be adjusted when they change. In Shelley's words, 'Nought may endure but mutability.' If the machinery is right the mutation will not prove too difficult. If it is wrong, it will provoke crises.

In addressing these difficult matters it is necessary to bear in mind the words of the original Schuman Declaration of 9 May 1950: 'Europe will not be made all at once according to a single general plan. It will be built through concrete achievements, which first create *de facto* solidarity.' Grand constitutional blueprints are not needed at this stage, nor are vast and far-reaching plans for co-operating first in one sphere and then in another. What is needed is machinery to enable a balance to be struck between national and Community powers so that those concrete achievements can be built up in a manner that reflects the member states' underlying needs, the realities of the moment and the wishes of the various electorates concerned. That is not an easy combination to reconcile.

The point about electorates needs emphasizing. Too often when Community procedures are discussed and mechanisms proposed for making them more efficient, it is forgotten that just as much as in the individual member states those who take decisions at the Community level must be accountable to those affected by them. Unless that fundamental democratic principle is respected Community procedures will not be able to produce decisions or, if they do, those decisions will be vulnerable to overturning at the national level.

In its early days that balance was struck by the Treaty of Rome itself. With its detailed instructions for establishing the Common Market and the Common Agricultural Policy and its deadlines for achieving those objectives the Treaty constituted a veritable programme for action. It was also a political bargain negotiated by governments to which the parties concerned all felt committed. They knew what they had let themselves in for and, equally important, the limits of their immediate liability. Naturally the original signatories had ambitions of their own that went beyond the short-term programme and these were by no means all the same; some were looking forward to a federal Europe, others had a quite different vision. But in the first instance all were operating on the basis of a programme that each one had individually accepted. Within this framework the Commission could bring forward proposals and the Council of Ministers take decisions.

The famous Paris Summit of 1972 tried to recreate such a programme. But because of the Yom Kippur War, the oil shocks and the recession that followed them, and because of the other problems then facing the Community, it failed. Since then there has been no established framework within which the member states and the Commission can work, and no point at which a balance can be struck between all the differing and conflicting interests to be found within the Community.

The result is chaos and irresponsibility. The Commission, the European Parliament and the individual member states all bring forward a constant stream of proposals of their own without there being any connecting thread between them. In the absence of an agreed overall view of how the Community should develop and what it should be trying to do, everyone not unnaturally pursues their own interests.

An additional complication arises from the nature of the Council of Ministers. In theory it is a single body; in fact it meets in a host of different 'formations' depending on the issues and ministers involved – Agriculture, Economic and Finance, Social Affairs, Industry, etc. and, supposedly directing them, the General Council which the Foreign Ministers attend. Just as there are rivalries between different ministers and departments in national governments, so these are reflected in the feelings the different formations of the Council have for each other. Moreover, each is inspired by the normal political desire to produce ambitious demands for action in its own particular field.

The consequence of all this is that the Community's decision-making machinery is permanently clogged by a vast mass of proposals, some going back a long way. The only ones that can be formally considered by the Council of Ministers are those submitted by the Commission, so that if the member states or the Parliament wish to get something formally on to the agenda of the Council they have to prevail on the Commission to put it forward. Three times a year the Commission publishes lists of all its outstanding proposals. These make remarkable reading. In June 1984, for instance, the total amounted to nearly 640 individual items, six of which dated from 1969 or earlier, and over 110 from 1978 or earlier. Decisions are arrived at rarely on the merits of an individual proposal, and usually only after complicated package deals have been laboriously stitched together covering a wide range of frequently unconnected items.

The lack of a framework for accepting or rejecting proposals on a continuing basis and the existence at any one time of a very large number of proposals, some of which are incompatible with each other, make financial planning, forecasting and discipline extremely difficult except through the imposition of cash limits in their crudest form. In agriculture the latter is often impossible, since once a guaranteed price has been set producers have the right to sell at that price to the intervention boards until either the price or the market regime is changed.

Serious as this situation is, it does not mean that the Community has ceased to function. The administration of the agriculture, social, regional, competition and other policies has continued and they have all evolved considerably over time. Annual budgets have been passed and implemented. The European Monetary System, the steel crisis regime and the Common Fisheries Policy have been introduced and carried into effect. Progress has been made in co-ordinating the foreign policies of the member states which has sometimes been impressive. The negotiations for a third Lomé Convention have been completed and the Community's development programme adjusted accordingly. The enlargement negotiations with Spain and Portugal have been brought to a successful conclusion. Life, in other words, has continued.

However, because the Community lacks a central point at which choices between different and rival options can be made and priorities set in an orderly and continuing fashion, a wholly disproportionate amount of effort and negotiation is required to achieve even the most modest progress. At its best the Community's advance resembles the celebrations that take place on Whit Tuesday every year at Echternach in Luxembourg; thousands of pilgrims approach the shrine of St Willibrord by means of a dance that involves taking two steps back for every three forward. At its worst it is even slower and more elaborate.

In a democracy, government is invariably an untidy business. It is necessary only to consider local government to recognize that. The larger the unit and the more diverse the range of interests to be reconciled, the untidier it tends to become, as the United States demonstrates. A political system made up of a collection of very different sovereign states is bound to face considerable and unusual difficulties. Neat, tidy and logical procedures would be impossible to administer unless supreme power was handed over to a central body, or one member was vastly stronger than the rest, neither of which would be desirable. When all is said and done, however, it is impossible to believe that the present Community system could not be made to work better.

Those who subscribe to the traditional orthodoxy would say at this stage that the remedy stares us in the face. So far as existing policies are concerned the Commission should revert to the arrangements laid down in the Treaty of Rome and demand a majority vote on its proposals whenever unanimity cannot be obtained. For the introduction of new policies the Treaty of

Rome demands unanimity, but those who regard themselves as cleaving closest to its spirit suggest that this rule should be relaxed. They also call for the role of the European Parliament to be enhanced. The majority of the members of the institutional affairs committee set up at Fontainebleau, and usually called the Dooge Committee after its Irish chairman, Senator James Dooge, reported along these lines.

There is much to be said for such an approach. But in their laudable desire to improve the efficiency of the Community's decision-making process its adherents overlook an essential point. It is the one made above; namely, that in the early days the Commission and the Council of Ministers were both working within a context established by governments. So too was the European Parliament, since at that time all its members were drawn from national parliaments, which had been required to ratify the treaty their governments had signed.

In those far-off days it was hoped by some that over time the Community institutions would themselves develop the political authority to become power centres in their own right. But de Gaulle's intervention and the other events already discussed stopped that from happening. They have developed in a different fashion, an examination of which will show that on its own the orthodox, or what might be termed 'treaty-plus', approach has no hope of success. It needs to be buttressed and contained within a new overall framework based on the European Council.

The Commission

It is appropriate to start any examination of the Community's institutions with the Commission. Its oddly shaped glass-fronted headquarters building, known as the Berlaymont after the convent and fashionable girls' school formerly on the site, symbolizes the Community to many people. The Commission's formal tasks are to submit proposals to the Council of Ministers, to execute and manage the policies decided upon by the Council, to represent the Community externally and to act as the guardian of the Treaty by ensuring that the member states observe its rules and principles and abide by the undertakings they have given in respect of its further development and the management of its policies.

As initiator, executive, sheriff and representative, the Commission's duty is to reflect the general interest in the welter of national ones. But as initiator it should be more than a mere signpost. It should act as the Community's intellectual leader, drawing the attention of the member states to new and more daring possibilities than they would otherwise envisage. The most notable recent example of the performance of this role was Roy Jenkins's speech at Florence on 27 October 1977, when he resurrected the idea of economic and monetary union and put forward proposals that, when taken up by Schmidt and Giscard d'Estaing, were implemented in modified form as the European Monetary System. The initial response in many parts of Europe to this initiative was mockingly dismissive, and courage was required to persevere with it. A more recent example is the setting of a 1992 target date for the elimination of all frontier obstacles within Europe, put forward by the present President, Jacques Delors, in January 1985.

The Commission also has another role that does not appear in the textbooks, but which arises out of its independent position and is extremely important. That is to act as a sort of permanent honest broker, problem solver and trouble-shooter. In that capacity it is the body to which others look to produce compromises, to break deadlocks and sometimes to determine whether a problem really exists as distinct from simply a complaint by an individual member state. Its 1979 report on the British budget problem, for instance, did exactly that. Nothing like the Commission can be found in the national life of the member states, and its responsibilities are more varied than those of other international bureaucracies.

In 1984 its staff numbered about 10,000 of whom about two-thirds were civil servants in the normally accepted sense of the word.* The rest were engaged in linguistic work of one sort or another; not for the Commission's own benefit, since it conducts its internal business mainly in French and to a lesser extent English, but for those in the member states who deal with it and expect everything it produces to be in their own language, which now means in nine versions. Whenever a minister or ambassador writes to the Commission he does so in his own language and expects a reply in the same, while citizens of member states naturally expect any proposal or decision that might have an impact on their lives to be available in their own language. The vast majority of Commission officials, who come from all the Community countries, join as a result of competitive examinations in their twenties and early thirties and stay for the rest of their lives, much like members of national bureaucracies – though special arrangements must, of course, be made to bring in people from the new member states whenever there is an enlargement. By the standards of national civil services the numbers employed by the Commission are modest. In 1983 the British civil service totalled 648,900. The figure for the Scottish Office was 13,100, for the Ministry of Agriculture, Fisheries and Food 12,700, for the Foreign and Commonwealth Office 11,100 and for the Treasury 10,600.

* There are also some 2,800 men and women employed by the Commission who are engaged on scientific research work at Ispra in Italy, Culham in Britain and other centres.

The role and responsibilities of the Commission and national bureaucracies are so different that they cannot, strictly speaking, be compared with each other. But because they come into contact with each other on such a continuous basis the comparison often is made. The Commission, it is said, is not as good as the French or British civil service, which are widely regarded as the best, but on a par with the second rank, and a good deal better than some. That in itself is a tribute when it is remembered that it has been going for only some thirty-five years and brings together so many cultural and linguistic traditions. The incoming commissioner quickly becomes accustomed to chairing meetings and leading negotiating teams every member of which may be of a different nationality. Outsiders, when they stop to think about it, find it amazing. Canadians and others engaged on the difficult task of trying to develop bicultural and bilingual institutions within a single country come to Brussels to see how it is done.

However, what especially marks the Commission off from any other institution, national or international, is the College of Commissioners itself and its constitutional status. Normally when governments and the media refer to the Commission this is the body they mean rather than the whole bureaucracy, and it is the one to which all the following remarks refer. The seventeen commissioners* – two each from Britain, France, Germany, Italy and Spain, and one each from the rest – are appointed for a four-year term by the Council of Ministers, which always accepts the nominees put forward by the national governments. They can be turned out of office only through a vote of censure by the European Parliament, and then only collectively. This puts the Commission in a most delicate position.

* Before the arrival of Spain and Portugal the number was fourteen.

Only by convincing the representatives of the member states in the Council of Ministers can it get its proposals translated into action, and only by sorting out their problems and differences can it break log-jams and deadlocks and get on with the management and development of existing policies. Yet its continued existence depends on the Parliament to which it must account for all its proposals and actions. It must, therefore, engage in a perpetual balancing act the difficulties of which are rarely appreciated by those who have not had to undergo the experience.

The Commission's internal arrangements are equally extraordinary, at least in British eyes. At first sight they look familiar as each commissioner has a responsibility or range of responsibilities – agriculture, external trade, competition, the budget, social affairs and so on – similar to those of ministers in a government. But there the similarity stops. In London the Prime Minister chooses his, or her, ministers, allocates their jobs and sacks or reshuffles them. Obviously the balance of power within the party and other considerations have to be taken into account, but there is no doubt who is the boss. The President of the Commission is in a very different position. Not only does he not choose his colleagues, nor have the power to sack them; he cannot even allocate their portfolios single-handedly. That is done by the Commission acting collectively on the basis of a proposal that he puts forward. Sometimes the process can be so fraught with personal and national rivalries that it can take days, as when Franco-Maria Malfatti took over in 1970. The two in which I participated in 1977 and 1981 both involved heated arguments round the Commission table and behind closed doors in the President's office, lasting in all for about twelve hours on each occasion as colleagues fought bitterly for position. This was despite the extensive preparatory talks conducted beforehand by Roy Jenkins and Gaston Thorn with the individuals concerned and their governments. Even when it is conducted without 'bloodshed', which Jacques Delors managed in 1985, the business is so complicated that reshuffles, apart from those attendant on the retirement of an individual or the arrival of new member states, have never so far been attempted.

In a British government everyone comes from the same party and they have known each other and worked together for all their political lives. Whatever their likes and dislikes, they are conscious of the fact that their personal fates are ultimately bound up with how the government as a whole and the party of which they are members perform. Their long-term interests are thus inseparably bound together regardless of their short-term rivalries. The members of the Commission are in a quite different position. They come from different national backgrounds and different political parties; when they leave Brussels they will go off in different directions. In these circumstances the President's task in moulding them into an effective team all aiming at the same objectives requires exceptional leadership and inspirational qualities.

When commissioners enter office they take an oath to be independent from all outside pressures, including those of national governments. At the same time they are drawn from the political life and often directly from the governments of the member states precisely in order that they should be able to bring their own political and national insights to bear on common problems. The Thorn Commission, in office from 1981 to 1985, included one ex-Prime Minister in Gaston Thorn himself and seven members who had at one time or another held cabinet posts in their own country. The present Delors Commission, which succeeded it, entered office with no less than four ex-Finance Ministers: Delors himself, Frans Andriessen from Holland, Henning Christophersen from Denmark and Willy de Clercq from Belgium. It is, moreover, not uncommon for incumbent commissioners to hold office in national party organizations in their home countries, as Guido Brunner did in the German Free Democrats during the Jenkins Commission. This apparent paradox of independence and involvement arises from a recognition of the fact that the European interest does not and cannot exist as something separate and distinct from that of the member states. It must, if it is to have any practical relevance, embrace the national interests of each of the member states and enhance their capacity for effective action.

To identify a European interest in these terms the Commission needs members who can explain and interpret their own countries in an authoritative fashion while showing understanding, in every sense of that word, for others. Their task should not be confused with that of national ministers or ambassadors. The ministers and ambassadors represent and must, if necessary, fight for their own national interest. The commissioner, by contrast, must seek to ensure that Commission proposals and compromises take fair and reasonable account of all such interests. Naturally he will be particularly concerned with those of 'the country he knows best', as the Brussels euphemism has it, but that must be within an overall European context. If his views are disregarded and he feels the final result is unfair, he is entitled to vote against. That will become known and in an important and controversial case will reduce the moral authority of the Commission initiative in question, sometimes to the point where it loses all validity. But if he is satisfied that the balance that has been struck is fair, taking into account the interests of others and the parameters of the debate, he should try to persuade his compatriots to support the Commission position and, failing that, to argue for it himself against the view of his national government.

To carry conviction with his Commission colleagues on the one hand and with his friends at home on the other he must remain plugged into the political life of his own country. But if he is thought by his colleagues to be simply an echo of what his home country government is saying he will lose their confidence, while if his friends at home think he has gone 'native', as it is sometimes put in London, he will lose theirs. The path through these minefields is not easy to follow and those who tread it must be prepared to risk a few explosions from either side.

Working on this basis the Commission achieves more than it is given credit for. Schmidt and Giscard d'Estaing are hailed as the fathers of the European Monetary System but, as has already been shown, they acted only after an initiative by Roy Jenkins on behalf of the Commission. The management of the steel crisis regime during my time in Brussels depended on the fair-mindedness and managerial ability of the Commission, and to a great extent on the flair of the responsible commissioner, Viscount Davignon. Throughout the long hard slog of the British budget problem the negotiations that led to each of the interim settlements and to the final one were preceded by Commission analyses and communications, which established the framework within which the member states worked, and pointed the way to the agreements that were reached. In 1985 it was the Commission, in its role of 'master of the compromise', which found a formula to end the dispute over the so-called 'Integrated Mediterranean Programmes'. This let the Greek Prime Minister, Andreas Papandreou, off the hook of his own demands and assuaged the economy-minded British and Germans, thereby removing the final obstacle to the conclusion of the enlargement negotiations with Spain and Portugal.

The President of the Commission has also acquired an international stature of an unusual nature. He attends all the proceedings of the European Council that involve the heads of state and government, which was not originally envisaged. He also, as a result of a tremendous battle for acceptance by Roy Jenkins in the late 1970s, attends the annual World Economic Summit along with the leaders of the United States, Japanese, Canadian, British, French, German and Italian governments.

This is a random list, drawn mostly from issues of which I have some personal experience, but it shows how effective the Commission can be. It also indicates, however, the limits of what it can hope to achieve, and why it cannot by itself be regarded as the engine of European unity and co-operation, as originally conceived.

One of these limits is inherent in the Commission's composition. By its nature it is a microcosm of the Community as a whole. Consequently when a position or point of view is held by the great majority of governments it tends to be regarded by the Commission as *communautaire*, while one that is held by only one or two governments tends to be regarded as 'national'. The Commission is at its best when there is a wide measure of agreement between the member states over ends and differences only on means. It can also be very good at reconciling two or more camps of roughly equal weight. But it has great difficulty in composing its internal differences to the point where it can act decisively in bringing together a large majority and a small minority. That is why the final stages of the British budget problem, after the Commission had done all the preparatory work and pointed the way to a settlement, could be successfully concluded only by the big three – President Mitterrand in the chair, Chancellor Kohl and Mrs Thatcher – acting together behind the scenes.

Another limitation on the Commission's ultimate capacity arises from its supranationality. On retiring from Brussels, one of the leading interpreters, Edmond Ferenczi, who came originally from Hungary, was asked what it was like not to have a country of his own to return to. In his reply he described the advantages of being open to a variety of different cultures and of being unblinkered by national prejudices. He then concluded, rather wistfully, by saying that 'a stateless person is like an acrobat working on a trapeze without a net'.[2]

That is very much the position of the Commission. In times of trouble governments can usually bank on their own supporters; and in the event of a dispute with another country, even a Community partner, their national public opinion as a whole can be expected to rally round. The Commission has no natural friends, and is invariably the scapegoat when things go wrong and difficult decisions have to be taken – such as, for instance, the imposition of milk quotas. That can be a useful function. Democratically elected governments often need outside agencies to blame when persuading their own people to take unpleasant but necessary medicine. But it is not a role that can be combined with the popular support needed to acquire real political authority.

The Commission also lacks the capacity to speak directly to the people of Europe over the heads of national governments, hard as it has tried. It is necessary only to compare the coverage accorded in Britain to Roy Jenkins when he was President of the Commission with what he subsequently received as one of the founders of the Social Democratic Party immediately on his return to grasp the nature of the problem. A comparison between the attention paid to Jacques Delors in France as Minister of Finance with what he now receives would yield a similar result. In countries other than their own it is even harder for the

President, let alone other members of the Commission, to attract attention.

This is not simply a matter of bad public relations, which a new consultant or more money could put right. It goes much deeper than that. National electorates and their media want to know above all what their elected representatives are doing, not about the activities of a collection of people, however wise and well intentioned, who are at best at one remove from them and who are not accountable to them. Those electorates do not accept that a body that has not been elected has the same right to be heard as those that have, or are seeking to be so. In modern Europe only the ballot box can confer political legitimacy and all that goes with it; nothing else can.

Consequently if the Commission is to be a real engine of unity and co-operation it must operate within the framework provided by an elective authority. In the 1960s when it was leading the member states towards the objectives set out in the Treaty it had that backing. Today it does not.

The European Parliament

In theory the European Parliament should be able to supply at least part of that framework since the introduction of direct elections in 1979. The existence of a parliamentary assembly elected by the people of Europe casting their votes for individuals and parties, rather than for national delegates, represents the ultimate embodiment of the European ideal. It is the antithesis of war and proof of the triumph of reconciliation. As such it demonstrates the continuing ambition to create a Community that transcends national frontiers.

Because of what it represents, statesmen from all over the world make the pilgrimage to Strasbourg: that city now in

France, so often in its history part of Germany, a symbol of Franco-German reconciliation, and the place where the European Parliament normally meets. Among the long and varied list of those from outside the Community who have addressed it are President Reagan of the United States, President Alfonsin of Argentina and the late President Sadat of Egypt. From within Queen Beatrix of Holland, President Mitterrand of France, President Pertini of Italy and Chancellor Kohl of Germany are among those to have done so. In addition to these ceremonial occasions it is customary for heads of government to make a report in person to the European Parliament after meetings of the European Council.

A man from Mars witnessing the State Opening of Parliament in London might be forgiven for supposing that power in the British political system resided with the Queen and the House of Lords rather than the members of the House of Commons summoned to stand and witness the proceedings. He would be likely to make a similar mistake if he visited the European institutions. The respect accorded to the Parliament by these visits and reports and the prestige of the ideal that it represents are not matched by the reality. For one thing, as pointed out in Chapter 1, the direct elections are European only in form. In practice they are so many national elections all taking place at the same time. For another, although it can sack the Commission and so exercise influence over that body, the powers of the European Parliament, like those of the House of Lords, are very limited.

In the Community system the Council of Ministers takes all the important decisions. The Parliament's role is largely consultative. Its opinion has to be sought on proposals submitted by the Commission to the Council, and the Commission usually accepts most of its amendments.

By delaying its opinion the Parliament can hold up a proposal that the Commission and member states wish to see brought forward, because the Council has to be in receipt of that opinion before itself reaching a decision. Like the delaying power of oppositions in national parliaments this weapon can be more powerful than it looks on paper. German members succeeded in holding up a Commission proposal to introduce freedom of service in insurance for some eighteen months, and there are numerous other examples of similar delays sometimes on behalf of national interests and sometimes for other reasons. This is an opportunity that lobbyists have not been slow to grasp and they can be very active – as, for instance, during the debates on the Commission's proposals to bring tobacco taxes into closer alignment, when representatives of both the multinational companies and the state-owned monopolies in France and Italy were very much in evidence. Once an opinion has been given, however, the Council is no more obliged to accept the Parliament's amendments to a Commission proposal than the original proposal itself, and the debate within the Council, in which the Commission participates and the Parliament does not, can quickly move in directions that were not anticipated when the amendments were tabled.

In the budget field the Parliament's powers are greater. Within certain fixed limits it can insist on increasing expenditure on non-agricultural policies through the annual budget, and if the budget as a whole does not meet with its approval it can reject it entirely. These powers have enabled the Parliament to engage in some notable and protracted disputes with the Council as well as the Commission, and sometimes to bring significant influence to bear. This was especially so when the annual rebates paid to the United Kingdom on its budget contribution formed part of the annual budget and were subject to parliamentary scrutiny.

Even these powers, though, are less than they seem, since if the budget is rejected, which has so far happened twice, no great crisis results. That of the previous year simply continues to apply hedged about by various restrictions until a new one is adopted. The European Parliament does not have the power either to withhold supply or to raise taxes, which is so central to the position of national parliaments.

Perhaps if prominent political personalities with established reputations and promising futures had been willing to serve in the European Parliament something could have been made of even these modest powers. But nowhere is the contrast between rhetoric and reality in Community affairs more apparent than on this point. Many such personalities have topped the lists of those elected under proportional representation in the member states, including François Mitterrand in 1979 before he became President, but few have then been prepared to devote much time to Strasbourg. Simone Veil of France is one of only a handful of exceptions. After a national election defeated ministers quite often take up seats in the European Parliament either by election or, as can be done in some countries, by replacing a retiring member. Sometimes they take their new responsibilities seriously. More often they treat the place as a convalescent home before returning to the national scene, as a launching pad for that purpose or as a form of retirement job like some British ex-cabinet ministers in the House of Lords.

The work of the House is done for the most part by men and women virtually unknown outside Strasbourg and the committee rooms of Brussels.* They receive scant thanks for their efforts, even in countries and parties that pride themselves on their Europeanism. Before the 1984 elections the leader of

* The Parliament's committees usually meet in Brussels.

the European People's Party, as the Christian Democrats call themselves at the European level, was an Italian, Paolo Barbi. It might have been thought that this would stand him in good stead at home so that he would get a sufficiently high place on the Italian Christian Democrat list to guarantee his re-election. But party headquarters in Rome had its own candidates for the best places and he did not return. Several other of the most prominent and active members from other countries were allocated places that either only just enabled them to squeeze back or led to their defeat. Even the President of the Parliament, Piet Dankert, had difficulty in securing the top position on the Dutch Socialist list. His robust approach to the deployment of American missiles played a part in this, but he had also 'been away too long' from domestic politics, as one of his compatriots put it. When Mitterrand formed his first government in 1981 he plucked Jacques Delors, who had previously had a very distinguished career outside elective politics, and Edith Cresson out of the Parliament, to become Minister of Finance and Minister of Agriculture respectively, which caused many MEPs to wonder whether perhaps their knapsacks too would contain a marshal's baton, but nothing comparable has happened since.

The sad truth is that it has proved almost impossible for members of the European Parliament to secure the public recognition that is indispensable to the creation of a political reputation and power base. In mid-1983 an opinion poll asked people in Belgium to name three of the country's MEPs. Forty per cent of the respondents could provide no answer, and among the seventy-one names mentioned only thirteen were members. The others were distinguished Belgians involved in European affairs, such as the Foreign Minister, Leo Tindemans, and the Vice-President of the Commission, Viscount Davignon.

It is hard to engage in politics if nobody seems very interested in what one is doing, and lack of public attention has led to large numbers of MEPs absenting themselves from the Parliament's proceedings, although the British members are among the most diligent. In recent years it has been rare for as many as 250 of the 434 members* to participate in a vote, and the number is often much less, for important as well as unimportant matters. Even the 'Draft Treaty Establishing a European Union', which represents the Parliament's blueprint for the future, attracted only 237 votes, with 31 against and 43 signifying their presence by recording an abstention. That was in February 1984. In April 1985, in the run-up to the Milan European Council, the Parliament returned to the question of European Union, and voted on two resolutions outlining the steps it wished to see taken to achieve that objective. One was carried with 202 votes for, 52 against and 30 abstentions; the other with 197 for, 41 against and 23 abstentions. The figures speak for themselves. They cannot be interpreted as the voice of the people issuing a resounding call to arms.

As might be expected when attendances are so poor, the Parliament finds it difficult on many subjects to sustain a consistent line of policy. The majority and therefore its position varies from one month to the next depending on who is present and which lobby among members is temporarily in the ascendant; one month it will be demanding restraint on agricultural expenditure and the next ever higher spending on the farming sector. In these circumstances the authority of its votes is still further reduced.

Despite these shortcomings the Parliament continues to harry the Commission, and the Commission devotes a good deal of

---

* This is the pre-enlargement figure. With the arrival of Spain and Portugal the number of members rose to 518.

effort to securing the Parliament's support and good opinion, and to trying to build up the importance of its activities. This is not simply because of the Parliament's powers of censure, though that plays a part. As a European body itself the Commission feels a collective responsibility to the European Parliament, and wants it to succeed. It also thinks that if the Parliament could become more influential that would be a useful counterweight to the power of the Council, which in turn would provide the Commission with more room for manoeuvre between the two institutions.

In addition there are often close links between individual commissioners and their party friends in the Parliament, with each trying to influence the other and the commissioners wanting to demonstrate their ability to translate their friends' desires into action, or at least into proposals, like any office-holding politician among his own supporters. These links were particularly close during the years 1981 to 1985 between the Christian Democrats in the two institutions. If a point was being pushed by members of that group in the Parliament one could be pretty sure that it would be taken up by the Christian Democrats in the Commission; while if the Christian Democrat commissioners were concerned about something, other commissioners could expect to be pressed on it in the Parliament. Those of us who did not have party colleagues in the Commission sometimes felt squeezed from both sides. The result of this complex set of relationships is that the natural desire of all elected representatives to promote legislation encourages the Commission to produce proposals over a wide area instead of concentrating on a short list of priorities.

If the relationship between the Commission and Parliament is characterized by a peculiar mixture of conflict and co-operation, that between the Parliament and the Council of Ministers is altogether more bland. Its failure to gain any real influence over the Council is one of the Parliament's biggest shortcomings. National parliaments call national ministers to account for what they have done in the national interest when they go to the Council of Ministers, and that is as it should be. The European Parliament is the place where the Council of Ministers as a whole, through its President, should be required to explain and justify what it has done, or failed to do, in the Community interest, but that hardly happens. It is true that there is nothing in the Treaty to say that it should, but equally there is nothing in the Treaty to prevent it, and it might be thought that elected representatives would have regarded it as one of their first priorities.

The role could have been developed either through the interrogation of the Council President on the floor of the House or, which would seem a more promising route, through congressional-type committee hearings held in public. There is a Question Time for the President of the General Council, but it is rarely treated as a major event, and national party political points and questions about emotive trouble spots in distant parts of the world, such as Nicaragua, tend to take up too much of its time. It can hold few terrors for any minister with experience of a national parliament. The committees rarely request the presence of ministers, and usually meet behind closed doors, which is not the way to attract attention nor to instil fear into the hearts of those called before them. Instead the Parliament has sought to exercise influence through gatherings at which a team of MEPs meets the Council or a delegation of ministers led by the President to thrash out a matter in private. A system has also been devised whereby the two bodies exchange views on various subjects on a similar basis at regular intervals. These tend to be stately, rather formal occasions which demonstrate a recognition by the Council of the Parliament's status, but rarely do much to influence ministers' subsequent actions.

The other area in which the directly elected European Parliament might have been expected to make an impact concerns political co-operation across frontiers. It has the potential to become a clearing house for political ideas on a Europe-wide basis, and the point at which like-minded parties co-ordinate strategies to be pursued simultaneously at European and national level. Although Christian Democrats, Socialists, Liberals and Communists sit together regardless of nationality while other parties that think they have something in common, like the Irish Fianna Fail and the French Gaullists, have formed joint groups, there has been little sign of this happening. Rather the reverse: instead of opening the way to a new form of pan-European politics, the European Parliament has tended increasingly to become a self-contained world of its own.

The outstanding example of an issue launched there being taken up by national parliaments and pursued simultaneously at European and national level is the clubbing to death of baby seals in Canada and the demand for a ban on the importation of certain Canadian seal products into Europe. The success of this campaign, which owed much to the Conservative MEP Stanley Johnson, who is no longer a member, shows that Europe-wide political action with the Parliament acting as a catalyst is possible. It would be much harder to mount on a less emotive and more politically divisive issue, but it is surprising all the same that so little has been done to develop the catalytic role.

It is still far too early to pass a definitive judgement on the European Parliament. The sheer practical problems involved in organizing an assembly composed of members from different national backgrounds and traditions were underestimated at the outset. They are bound to take a long time to straighten out, and even longer will be required for the institution to establish effective working methods. Meanwhile the strength of feeling in several member countries in favour of the ideal the Parliament represents, and the awareness in all that its collapse would be seen as a blow to the credibility of the Community itself, will ensure that continued attempts are made to enhance its reputation and to find it a more satisfying role. The Parliament itself may seek to accelerate the process by some dramatic gesture, such as sacking the Commission, a possibility that members constantly discuss among themselves.

However, neither the conferment from above of additional powers, which are bound to be modest, nor dramatic gestures will bring about any real change until the underlying causes of the Parliament's present *malaise* have been tackled. More prominent political personalities must serve there, it must find ways of calling the Council publicly to account, it must be able to maintain consistent majorities in favour of consistent policy objectives and it must become a catalyst for Europe-wide political action. Until at least some of these things are done it will remain a marginal influence on European affairs, suffering from what one of my colleagues used to call an 'existenz *angst*'.

The Council of Ministers

The hub of Community affairs is to be found in a slab-like anonymous building, next door to the Berlaymont in Brussels, called the Charlemagne where the Council of Ministers meets.* When it is in session – and in its various formations it meets more than eighty times a year,† usually for a day, sometimes for

---

* In April, June and October, however, the Council always meets in Luxembourg.
† That was the case in 1983 and 1984. In earlier years it was rather less.

two and occasionally for longer – the ground floor may be thronged with journalists. But the real work takes place on the fourteenth floor where the conference rooms are. The three lifts that serve it are hopelessly inadequate for a big occasion. Foreign Ministers, Finance Ministers, officials, interpreters, secretaries and messengers all crowd in, exchanging greetings in every language. Once arrived, however, ministers and commissioners move into a fast stream. Although all are supposed to carry passes, the security men pride themselves on being able to distinguish the famous sheep from the unknown goats so that the former can sweep unchecked into the conference rooms while their assistants are held back.

In fact it is those whose faces would not be known outside the Charlemagne who frequent the building most often. Some indeed spend most of their days there. They are the officials of the national missions, known as Permanent Representations, accredited to the Community, who form a hierarchy of committees to prepare the meetings of the Council of Ministers. The most important are the 'permanent representatives' themselves, who are invariably senior ambassadors and whose committee is known as Coreper after its French initials. In some weeks it may meet several times as its members try to thrash out compromises for ministers to approve and to identify the main points at issue on which the Council should concentrate. In theory it deals with all the most important subjects, but the range and complexity of matters coming before the Council are so great that their deputies usually take on a number while the agriculture counsellors, who all originate from ministries of agriculture, form a special group to prepare Agriculture Councils.

The theory is that experienced diplomats operating behind the scenes and without the glare of publicity can deal more smoothly with contentious and difficult points than their political masters. As a result of their work, therefore, rows should be avoided and agreements reached more easily than would otherwise be the case. Sometimes this is how things work out in practice, but not always. As long ago as 1919 when the League of Nations was being set up, Sir Alexander Cadogan, who later became head of the Foreign Office from 1938 to 1946, warned of the dangers inherent in a system of permanent representatives. They might well, he felt, become a corps of professional debators, carrying out their instructions to the letter and developing obstruction into a fine art.[3] When complex and intractable problems arise in the Community the 'perm reps' in Brussels are apt to fall into that trap. They are also prone to develop titanic personal rivalries of which the most notable during my period was that between the British Sir Michael Butler and his French opposite number, Luc de la Bar de Nanteuil. It became one of the features of Brussels life, to be followed and discussed like the constantly repeated battles on the international tennis circuit between Martina Navratilova and Chris Lloyd.

Council meetings always begin, and often continue, in a formal setting. Ministers and their top advisers, including the 'perm reps', sit in alphabetical order by country round a large rectangular table with junior officials behind them, and the national delegation holding the presidency and the Commission facing each other at either end. When the subject under discussion is particularly sensitive or confidential, or when the going gets rough, the presidency will often suggest that 'only ministers plus two', or even only one, should stay, and perhaps also move the meeting to a smaller and more intimate room. In exceptional circumstances only ministers and commissioners are allowed to participate, though when that happens those ministers with the most problems are generally allowed one helper. On one such occasion I remember spending nine continuous hours in a small room with 'ministers and commissioners only' as Geoffrey Howe, for the umpteenth time, played the role of Horatius holding the British bridge on the budget problem against all his colleagues. When Sir Michael Butler took up a discreet position in one corner, from which he proceeded to pass notes to his minister, the French Foreign Minister, Roland Dumas, summoned one of his officials to sit in another. Honour was satisfied and the meeting proceeded. The alternative would have been for Sir Michael to leave the room.

The other standard tactic in times of trouble is for the meeting to be adjourned and for the President, accompanied by the commissioner concerned and one or two officials, to hold 'confessionals' with the heads of each delegation in turn. When it is the President's own national delegation that is holding up an agreement his position can be horribly difficult. A big man can turn it to advantage. During the worst of the troubles over the establishment of a Common Fisheries Policy, when Denmark was in a minority of one, I, as acting President of the Commission in Gaston Thorn's absence, worked closely in a Fish Council with Henning Christophersen,* then the Danish Finance Minister and in the chair while the Danish Minister of Fisheries took the national seat. Thanks to his personal authority and fair-mindedness we nearly made a breakthrough. But it has to be said that not all Council Presidents in such a position play the game in quite the same way.

Lunch is an important part of any Council meeting. It is invariably lavish and prolonged, and only ministers and the commissioners concerned attend, plus two or three officials to help the President and keep a record. Whereas in the formal

---

* Currently my successor as Vice-President of the Commission responsible for the budget.

proceedings everyone insists on speaking his own language, at lunch all make a big effort to use French or English with only those who absolutely cannot being accompanied by interpreters. The conversation is free and intimate – often astonishingly so. Geoffrey Howe frequently points out that in some months he sees more of his opposite numbers in the Council of Ministers than of his national colleagues in the cabinet, taking into account the variety of European and other international meetings they all attend. It is at Council lunches and other informal gatherings that the effect of this on their personal relationships becomes apparent.

At a typical Finance Ministers' lunch the discussion might range over such subjects as recent individual contacts with the Americans, exchange rates, preparations for forthcoming international meetings, which European candidate to back for a high position at the International Monetary Fund or some other international body, and the latest twist in the Latin American debt saga. Before a World Economic Summit ministers from those states that do not attend will take the opportunity to press their views on those that do. Sometimes a minister may also sound out his colleagues on ideas circulating within his own government or give advance warning of something that is about to happen.

The Council's *modus operandi* places great demands on ministers. They are always in the ring and sometimes their assistants are not even in the corner. Consequently those with a genuine command of their subject, able to speak and known to do so for their governments, and with the self-confidence to adapt their positions, have a great advantage over those without these attributes. The ability to think quickly and to convince or overbear colleagues is also important.

Among the most effective British performers in my eight years were Denis Healey, Lord Carrington, Peter Walker and Geoffrey Howe. Even when Geoffrey Howe was going through some of his worst periods in the House of Commons his infinite patience, command of detail, patent goodwill and conversational manner were highly effective in the very different conditions of the Council. As Foreign Secretary in the Callaghan government David Owen was handicapped by obviously not being in a position to 'deliver' his government; and the fact that everyone knew that Francis Pym was at odds with Mrs Thatcher served to reduce his effectiveness. By the same token the present French Foreign Minister, Roland Dumas, who is known to be very close to President Mitterrand, possesses a weight his predecessor, Claude Cheysson, lacked. When a minister commands great political influence at home plus long experience of the Council the combination can be very powerful. Josef Ertl, who as German Agriculture Minister sat for thirteen years in his Council, is one example of that, and his compatriot Hans-Dietrich Genscher, who in 1984 completed ten years in the Foreign Ministers' Council, is another.

Like the Commission, the Council's weaknesses are inherent in its composition. The most obvious is that in whatever formation it is meeting – Foreign Minister, Finance, Agriculture, Industry, etc. – the members are far from being equal. Some carry clout, others do not. Those who do not find it very hard to deviate from their brief and so to clinch an agreement in anything other than 'pre-cooked' conditions. In any case, if an item is politically sensitive at home a subordinate minister, even one as important as a Foreign, Finance or Agriculture Minister, will be reluctant to incur the odium of making a concession if he can get the matter referred to the heads of state and government in the European Council. This tends to be particularly so when a subordinate minister is from a different party in a coalition than his Prime Minister and sees party as well as political advantage in passing the poisoned chalice to his boss.

Another problem arises from the Council's practice of meeting in different formations. There is no alternative. If everything had to be done by some specially constructed group of Euro-ministers, the range of subjects would be too great for any individual to master and the agenda so long that their meetings would be endless. But, under the present arrangement, there is always a possibility that the work of one Council will be undone by another.

A well-publicized example of this occurred in the early days of October 1984. On the evening of Monday the 1st the Finance Ministers reached the verge of agreement on a new and long-overdue system of budgetary discipline for the Community. No sooner had their meeting finished, and the news spread to a nearby room where the Agriculture Ministers were in session, than the French Farm Minister, Michel Rocard, told the press that the Finance Ministers, including his own colleague Pierre Bérégovoy, were trying to 'strangle the common agricultural policy'.[4] Other less outspoken Farm Ministers shared his indignation. The following day the Foreign Ministers refused to accept what the Finance Ministers had done; the German Foreign Minister, Hans-Dietrich Genscher, going so far as to denounce it as 'anti-discipline' despite the endorsement of his finance colleague, Gerhard Stoltenberg.[5]

Such disputes are not usually so highly publicized nor fast moving as this, but the danger of Councils cutting across each other is a constant one. Where expenditure policies other than the Common Agricultural Policy are concerned, the outcome is often finally determined in the Budget Council. It is there that Treasury Ministers, whose national colleagues in the Energy, Industry or Social Affairs Councils may have produced high sounding ideas and indicated support for far-reaching Commission proposals, can reassert the power of the purse by agreeing to only the minimum possible expenditure levels. In the case of agriculture, where expenditure flows directly from policy decisions, control is harder to exert and it remains to be seen whether the new budgetary discipline arrangements finally agreed in 1984, despite Michel Rocard's anger, will enable the Finance Ministers to establish a framework within which the Agriculture Ministers can be contained.

A third difficulty arises from the sheer complexity of bringing ten ministers from ten governments, let alone twelve in future, to the point of agreement. When eventually it has been reached, so many interconnecting compromises and concessions have been made that the final result is liable to be set in concrete. If the issue in question is purely internal that may be a good thing. But when it concerns the position the Community is to take up in an international negotiation it can give rise to considerable problems. It means either that the Commission, on behalf of the Community, has to be completely unyielding or that it has to return to the Council and start off yet another round of internal negotiations whenever the state of the external one alters. The main reason why the last stages of the enlargement negotiations with Spain and Portugal were so protracted was not because of the difficulties between those two countries and the Community, but because it took the member states so long to reach common positions.

In theory Foreign Ministers in the General Council are supposed to exercise a general direction over all the others and to play a supervisory role. But their capacity to do so is limited since they are by no means necessarily more important in their own governments than their ministerial colleagues. Indeed, they often have less political weight in their own capitals than those who speak on behalf of powerful sectional interests, such as agriculture or industry. It is simply not realistic to suppose that they can set objectives that others will feel bound to follow, or arbitrate in the case of disputes between other Councils. Only the heads of state and government in the European Council can do that. Moreover, so far as public opinion is concerned, transferring a disputed and controversial issue from one Council of Ministers to another signifies very little. It is only by moving it up to the European Council that those whose interests are at stake – farmers, fishermen, steel companies and their workers, for example – can be convinced that everything possible is being done to defend their position or find a solution, as the case may be.

Nor is qualified majority voting in the Council of Ministers the *deus ex machina* that so many seem to believe.* The way it is often discussed and advocated might lead the uninitiated to suppose that its introduction would represent some entirely new and bold initiative, a return to the Treaty that would simultaneously mark a great leap forward.

In fact the various stages whereby the Budget Council deals with the annual budget have been conducted by majority voting for many years. Votes have even taken place in other Councils more often than is realized without creating a fuss. The experience has not been encouraging. The Budget Council never attempts to move beyond the lowest common denominator of possible agreement around the table. It has no sense of overall framework nor of ultimate objectives. Everything is done in the

---

* The word 'qualified' is important. The voting is not done on the basis of one country, one vote. The votes are weighted so that the large have more than the small. Britain, France, Germany and Italy have 10 each. Spain has 8, Belgium, Greece, Holland and Portugal 5, Denmark and Ireland 3 and Luxembourg 2. Out of a total of 76, 54 are needed to constitute a majority.

same *ad hoc* fashion that has characterized all the Community's activities in recent years. When votes occur in the other Councils they remove individual boulders from the Community's path here and there, but bring about no tangible improvement in the overall situation.

Yet it is easy to understand why the idea of majority voting retains a hold on the imaginations of so many who feel frustrated by the Community's record in recent years. The search for unanimity has proved so difficult as to render agreement almost impossible. When on top of that a government has only to indicate that it will invoke a vital national interest when it does not like the way a discussion is proceeding, whatever chance of success there may have been can disappear. In such circumstances it is natural to suppose that an arrangement is needed whereby the talking can be brought to a stop and decisions taken. If everyone could be relied on to accept the outcome, such a procedure would indubitably speed matters up.

It is at this point, however, that the political realities within the member states must be taken into account. There is first of all the position of the government or governments that have been defeated to consider. If a government has taken a public stand against a particular proposal in Brussels, can it be expected to turn round and support that proposal within its own country after being defeated in the Council? Such a manoeuvre would in any circumstances be difficult to execute and involve a terrible loss of prestige. If, as is quite possible, it led to the government's downfall and replacement by a new administration that also opposed the majority decision of the Council of Ministers, then that decision would become inoperable in the country in question. It would not necessarily require a very important issue or rebuff to bring such a situation about. Much that is decided upon in Brussels requires action by national parliaments to bring it into effect, so that even a small matter could force a government to seek parliamentary approval for an about-turn.

Secondly, there is the principle of democratic accountability, which lies at the heart of the political systems of all member states. It would be contrary to that principle for governments that had not been elected by the people of country X to impose a decision on them that had been opposed by their own elected government. In any case, in the real world, as distinct from that of constitutional theorizing, there is no way in which that can be done in a Community of free and equal sovereign nations.

None the less, there is a way forward. If the member states at the highest political level can agree on the specific objectives they wish to pursue in specific policy areas then majority voting can be used as a means to attain those objectives. In other words majority voting is feasible and consistent with democratic principles, if it is used as an administrative and management tool within an agreed political framework to which the member states have explicitly committed themselves. It is not feasible nor consistent with those principles as a device for establishing political objectives in the first place.

This is indeed the principle on which the Community was based in its early days. Objectives were set out in the Treaty, to which all governments subscribed, and majority voting was laid down as a means to attain them. In the case of policies that had not been established by the Treaty, the Treaty itself specifically states in Article 235 that unanimity is required. The words of that article are worth spelling out in full: 'If action by the Community should prove necessary to attain, in the course of the operation of the Common Market, one of the objectives of the Community, and this treaty has not provided the necessary powers, the Council shall, acting unanimously on a proposal from the Commission and after consulting the Assembly, take the appropriate measures.' Thus the Treaty clearly recognizes that majority voting cannot be used as a means whereby individual member states can be forced by others to pursue goals that were not agreed at the outset.

There are those who argue that the road round this article and the constitutional doctrine it embodies lies through the European Parliament. Now that the Parliament is elected by the people of Europe – so the argument goes – it should be entitled to a greater say in determining a general European interest and in the law-making process. In its own 'Draft Treaty Establishing a European Union' the Parliament suggests the phasing out of the right of member governments to invoke a vital national interest and a procedure whereby laws binding on the member states should be enacted by the Council, using majority voting, and the Parliament together and, if the Council cannot take a vote, by the Parliament alone. In present circumstances, however, such a proposition is divorced from reality.

The European Council

Only one body exists that can establish new goals and political objectives, and lay down guidelines for how problems, internal and external, should be approached on a continuing basis. That is the European Council. The heads of state and government that make it up represent the supreme political authority in contemporary Europe. Whether they are directly responsible to the people, like the French President, or indirectly so, for as long as they command a majority in their national parliaments it is on their desks that the political buck finally stops. It is to them and to the governments they lead that the people in all the member states look for the big decisions and it is they who are finally held responsible for what happens.

Others can launch ideas and initiatives, prepare the work of
the European Council and seek to guide its members in their
deliberations. The Commission as guardian of the general interest has a crucial role to play. If it is both imaginative and far-
sighted there is no reason why it should not from time to time
lead the heads of state and government in directions they had
not expected, as Roy Jenkins did over the European Monetary
System. In any event it must feel free to make whatever proposals
it thinks fit. But only the heads of state and government can
strike a final balance between different and conflicting interests,
establish goals and set guidelines within which the member
states and Community institutions must work. If they cannot,
or will not, nobody else can. The responsibility is not one that
can be delegated.

The European Council is not mentioned in the Treaty of Rome
and grew up later. As a result there are some who argue, even
now, that it has no proper place in Community proceedings and
is some sort of constitutional aberration. Such a proposition is
self-evidently absurd and in any case Jean Monnet, a supremely
practical man if ever there was one, himself wanted heads of
state and government to be directly involved in European affairs
and played a significant role behind the scenes in helping to
launch the Summit meetings that evolved into the European
Council. When that happened, as a result of an initiative by
President Giscard d'Estaing, he wrote to the President that 'the
creation of the European Council is the most important decision
for Europe since the Treaty of Rome'.[6]

The subsequent career of the European Council has not lived
up to this accolade. It has too often become bogged down in the
details of internal disputes that should have been settled by
subordinate ministers and for which it becomes a court of
appeal. The British budget problems and, more recently, Greece's

demands for special treatment provide classic examples of this. It has also too often succumbed to the temptation of issuing high-sounding declarations that indicate concern but give no clear policy guidance on the matters that have engaged its attention. The list of examples here is legion, ranging from energy, when there was fear of a shortage, to the handling of unemployment. The impression is created that decisions in principle have been taken and that action will follow, but frequently the basis for such action has not been created and no follow-up actually occurs.

The European Council meets three times a year: once in Brussels or Luxembourg, and once in each of the two countries holding the six-monthly rotating presidency. The participants normally assemble in time for lunch or in the early afternoon of the first day and depart during the afternoon of the second, though sometimes they have to stay until well into the evening. The morning of the second day is normally a key session so that lunch may not be taken till tea-time, and afternoon in any case becomes evening. On one occasion, as the morning session dragged on towards 3.30 p.m., the Belgian Prime Minister, Wilfried Martens, was heard to remark that no Belgian could wait beyond four o'clock for his lunch and the President was prevailed upon to bring matters to a close. The occasions combine the characteristics of an intimate gathering and a mass reunion in a manner that is all their own.

At the heart are the meetings of the heads of state and government themselves. These are very intimate affairs being attended only by the leaders and their Foreign Ministers plus the President of the Commission and one of his Vice-Presidents – besides, of course, the inevitable interpreters in their booths around the walls. At the London meeting in 1981 when the French Minister for Europe, André Chandernagor, was jostling for position with the Foreign Minister, Claude Cheysson, he joined the French party at Lancaster House, but was not allowed into the meeting room. Officials are sternly excluded, except for three to help the presidency and record a master minute, and one per delegation who can run in and out with messages but not stay. The absence of officials is supposed to enable the politicians to speak more freely together, but can also lead to misunderstandings as not all the Prime Ministers and Foreign Ministers are equally good at following what is happening, keeping a note or remembering it afterwards. The informal proceedings and some of the meals are even more restricted, with just heads of government and the President of the Commission present, and those who can do without interpreters.

The intimacy of the meetings does not necessarily make for good relations. Heads of government are by definition accustomed to being in command of their surroundings. At home they preside over their cabinets and, even if some are no more than *primus inter pares*, they are for the most part not used to being simply one of the *pares*. Yet at the European Council that is what they are. The task of the President in leading the discussion and securing agreements is not easy, especially if he is from a small country and lacks experience. Sometimes men labouring under both handicaps rise to the occasion. On others they do not. The tone of the exchanges can be very forthright, and those who feel that they have more power and influence than the rest do not hesitate to try to secure advantages.

National differences can also be compounded by personal ones. Those between Schmidt and Giscard d'Estaing on the one hand and Mrs Thatcher on the other have already been recounted. On another occasion Mrs Thatcher and Charles Haughey were asked to share an interpreter at meal-times, which meant sitting next to each other. Anglo-Irish relations as well as those between the two leaders were at a particularly low ebb at the time and she refused. On top of that the leaders' press officers and entourages can intensify latent hostilities and even create annoyances without it ever being quite clear whether they are operating on their own initiative or at the behest of their superiors. On one notably ludicrous occasion the background briefing coming from the British camp likened Mrs Thatcher's stand on the issue under discussion to the squares formed by the British infantry at the Battle of Waterloo and their success at repelling the French cavalry charges. The French responded with references to the burning of Joan of Arc. Whether they meant that Mrs Thatcher should suffer the same fate, or that her activities were comparable with those responsible for the martyrdom, I never discovered.

Each head of state and government comes with a retinue of officials and specialists. The political directors, who are very senior officials from the various Foreign Offices, are often required to prepare the Political Co-operation aspects of the talks. Others, including the ubiquitous 'perm reps', are sometimes needed to deal with particular points of difficulty or new problems that emerge during the meeting. They may also become involved in endless haggling over the drafting of the communiqué or be needed for the various bilateral meetings between individual leaders, like those of Mrs Thatcher and Garret Fitzgerald, that invariably take place *en marge* of a European Council. Often though they give the impression – and this applies to all nationalities – of being there primarily to demonstrate their indispensability. At Dublin in 1979 five Whitehall knights were at one time to be seen seated together on a bench for hours on end like so many patients waiting to be summoned into the doctor's presence.

The range of subjects covered at a European Council can be

very wide, far wider than the scope of the Treaty. There is invariably a discussion of the economic and social situation within the Community on the basis of a Commission report, and on whatever topical issues – political, economic and even security-linked – the leaders think important or one of them wishes to raise. Special attention may be paid to some aspect of some internal Treaty-based policy, such as the development of the internal market, or to some common problem, such as youth unemployment or the development of new technologies. Declarations are issued setting out the Community's position on international problems that are causing concern, such as Poland, Afghanistan or Lebanon, and reviews are undertaken of such internal matters as the negotiations for establishing a Common Fisheries Policy at one moment, the enlargement negotiations with Spain and Portugal at another, and the development of the Community and the reform of its institutions at a third. Not all the items that appear in the final communiqué are necessarily handled by the heads of state and government. Some may be dealt with by the Foreign Ministers or officials in hastily assembled meetings taking place at the same time and rubber-stamped by the leaders in agreeing the communiqué. But any or all of them can be taken over by the leaders themselves, and anything done within the overall scope of their meetings and recorded in the final communiqué engages their responsibility.

The subjects discussed at a European Council and the content of the subsequent communiqué are by no means necessarily synonymous. Exchanges of view almost invariably take place on matters that find no place within it or go much further than the communiqué indicates. They may be of a purely reflective nature or part of a long-term process of policy formulation. Either way these informal unreported exchanges play an important part in bringing the minds of the leaders and their governments closer together and helping to create the springs from which common European attitudes, approaches and positions may subsequently flow.

The time has now come for the European Council to take a decisive step forward and become the central point at which choices are made and priorities set. It won't be easy, as this account of its activities shows, though it should not be more difficult for some of the leaders than working in a national coalition. Like any other political system the Community must have a central authority. As long ago as 1974 Jean Monnet told Giscard d'Estaing, 'what's lacking more than anything else in European affairs is authority. Discussion is organized: decision is not.'[7] He hoped the European Council would fill the void. It is now time that it did so in a manner consistent with contemporary realities. As a first step it should formally undertake responsibility for establishing an agenda on the basis of which all member states can work, a framework within which European co-operation can be conducted and a machinery for following up what has been decided.

The Need for an Agenda

This agenda would have two inspirations. One is the action programme contained in the Treaty of Rome. In a sense it would represent the modern equivalent of that. The other is the agreements that political parties reach before forming governments in those countries where coalitions are the normal practice. Those parties all have their own short-term objectives and long-term aspirations. But they recognize that for as long as they are in harness together they must have a common programme and a common view on how to tackle the problems facing their country. Inevitably as with those coalition programmes, no member state would get all it wants. Some objectives would have to be set aside until circumstances and/or governments in other countries change. Even so, as in the early days of the Community everyone would know what they have agreed to try to achieve and the limits of their liability. A framework would also have been established within which detailed problems of management and execution could be hammered out.

To work in a Community context such a programme would require certain special features. In a national situation coalitions can break down and the parties concerned form new alliances with others who until recently were their opponents. In Germany, for example, where coalition programmes are exceptionally detailed and can run to over forty pages of text, the Free Democrats were still able to jump from the Socialist to the Christian Democrat bed with hardly a pause for breath. In the Community that is not possible. The member states have committed themselves to a catholic marriage. The terms and conditions of the action programme must take account of that.

One consequence is that it should be established on a rolling basis; that is to say, renewed and adjusted as the case may be to take account of changing circumstances. On a regular basis – say, once a year or once every two years – the European Council would agree to a set of objectives for the Community to work towards during the period ahead and the guidelines for dealing with current problems, both internal and external. Where appropriate deadlines would be set, but this would not always be the best way to proceed. The European Council's present schedule of three meetings a year should provide ample scope to monitor progress and make sure that its instructions are being followed, though the duration of some of them would have to be extended. From time to time it will wish to push things along faster than they are going, and on others to make adjustments in the light of unexpected difficulties. Its communiqués and the 'invitations' to the Council of Ministers which it already issues will enable it to do so.

Inevitably disputes will arise between member states about what was originally intended and how it should be attained. After every European Council there are subordinate ministers and officials who feel that 'my man' (or 'woman') did not achieve all he should or play his cards quite right. Accordingly they try to pull things back in the Council of Ministers, official working parties and wherever else they can. Moreover, quite apart from these problems, which are typical of bureaucratic life the world over, the European Council cannot be expected to do more than establish a framework. The individual Councils of ministers – Agriculture, Economic and Finance, Internal Market and above all General – must fill in the details, which are bound to require much negotiation and argument.

In most cases the co-ordination and guidance role should be given to the Foreign Ministers meeting in the General Council. As they attend the European Council and are responsible under present arrangements for its preparation it makes sense for them also to take charge of the follow-up, including the reconciliation of differences between countries and Councils. It is, however, essential for them to receive an explicit mandate from the heads of state and government otherwise they will not be able to assert themselves against other ministers.

In addition it will in some cases be necessary for the European Council to stipulate that one specialist Council should operate within guidelines laid down by another. That should certainly be so for Agriculture on the one hand and Economic and Finance on the other. The Agriculture Ministers should continue to be responsible for all aspects of agricultural policy, but they should operate within a financial framework laid down by their Finance Minister colleagues. That is how spending ministers have to operate within the individual member states and unless similar working methods can be established in the Community it will be impossible ever to organize the CAP on a rational basis. This innovation, which is very much in line with the ideas on budgetary discipline that have been evolving in the Community in recent years, will be difficult to implement. Agriculture Ministers will fight for their continued independence, while some Finance Ministers will be very reluctant to incur the odium that will arise in their home countries from being seen to be part of the body that is limiting agricultural expenditure. Nothing could more vividly illustrate the need for the heads of state and government to lay down priorities and the means to secure them.

Within the various Councils majority voting should be a normal procedure on all matters flowing from the objectives set and guidelines established by the European Council. It should never be regarded as something that is good in itself. Every effort should always first be made to secure a consensus since that must be the best way to proceed where sovereign states are concerned, just as it is when different language or religious groups are involved within a single country. When a government has genuinely serious problems it should have the opportunity to delay a decision for a reasonable amount of time so that the search for an agreement acceptable to all may continue. On the other hand there must be safeguards against filibustering as well. The procedures necessary to reconcile these conflicting requirements need not be complicated, but they must be clear to all.

Once again it is necessary that one Council should be seen to be in charge, and in this case it should be the General Council as part of its overall responsibility for the follow-up to the European Council's decisions. When a minister invokes a vital national interest to hold up a decision in a specialist Council the Foreign Minister of that country should be obliged to explain the reasons why in the General Council, and a time limit should be set for sorting the matter out. Thus, under this system when Ignaz Keichle invoked a German vital national interest in the Agriculture Council to prevent a cut in cereal prices in 1985, the German Foreign Minister, Hans-Dietrich Genscher, would have been called upon to explain why in the General Council. To overcome the current irresponsibility and chaos of the decision-making procedures in the Community not only should there be a central authority but those who participate in it should be obliged to ensure that their own ministers pursue mutually compatible objectives within each of the specialist Councils. If Foreign Ministers were forced to make explanations of the sort suggested on behalf of their masters it would spur governments to get their own internal priorities straight, which the German government, with its devotion to budgetary stringency on the one hand and to high cereal prices on the other, had obviously failed to do in 1985.

If it becomes apparent that the disputes are so great and deep-seated that the agreement reached at the European Council has, in effect, broken down then the whole matter will have to be referred back to heads of state and government. But that should be a quite exceptional procedure resorted to only in cases of dire necessity. The European Council must not become a constant court of appeal or it will not be able to concentrate on the task of setting the course for others to follow, which only it can do.

At the subordinate level of the Council of Ministers the rules for taking decisions can be placed within the overall framework of the European Council and derived from it. But that still leaves the problem of how to bring about a common position among the heads of state and government. That is bound to be difficult. They epitomize the very real differences that exist between the member states, and their responsibilities as well as the multiplicity of conflicting domestic pressures that are brought to bear on each combine to drive them apart. To suggest that this problem can be overcome by the simple expedient of a majority vote is absurd. As has already been said, in a Community of free and equal sovereign nations it could not be enforced. Nor is there any other 'quick fix' that can be applied. If a small group of large countries were to try to impose its will on the rest the system would break apart, and the same would happen if a self-appointed 'in-group' of large and small countries were to make the same attempt. There will always be some countries, like Ireland and Italy at the outset of the European Monetary System, that will rather jump aboard a train getting up steam than be left at the station. But there are equally likely to be others that will resist all efforts to bundle them aboard, like Britain on the same occasion.

Concentric Circles

This brings us to the second great difference that there will have to be between a national and a Community coalition programme. In the Community not all member states can be expected to do everything at the same time and in the same manner. They cannot even be expected to undertake the same commitments. It is hard to imagine a coalition in national politics working well for any length of time, even with very limited objectives, with as many as twelve participating parties. When twelve countries are involved the problems are far more complex. In any circumstances it would be extremely difficult to reconcile their positions. But when the differences in their characters, economic and social structures and political aspirations are as wide as those that now exist within the Community the task becomes monumental.

This is not a novel point. The recent increase in the number of members represents a change of degree rather than of kind. In the 1970s Ralf Dahrendorf and Willy Brandt both suggested that the Community might work better if it did not insist on too much uniformity, and several others produced ideas along the same lines. Since then, as was described in Chapter 1, some of the most striking initiatives have in fact been on a partial rather than a unanimous basis, involving some but not all member states. The European Monetary System and the later stages of the economic sanctions against Argentina at the time of the Falklands crisis are two within the Community framework which come readily to mind. Outside it there are a number in the industrial field, of which the Tornado military aircraft, the Airbus and the Ariane rocket project are perhaps the best known.

Like so much else in contemporary Europe this development has taken place in an *ad hoc* fashion without any guiding principle. It is easy to understand why governments that want to go ahead with a new initiative – be it closer co-operation in a policy field, or a common project – become impatient if the interests and hesitations of others seem likely to hold them back. Moreover bringing others in may not just delay an initiative's implementation; it may dilute the prospective gains of the original movers as well. On the other side if something gets under way that causes domestic problems in a particular member state, the government of that member state may find it easier to stand on the sidelines than to try to change the views and prejudices of its own public opinion. That could well be the case with Ireland on any matter touching on security.

These are practical points which at any given moment, under the pressure of events, may well weigh more heavily with busy ministers and officials than abstract notions of Community orthodoxy. Yet in this area those notions deserve more attention than they are accustomed to receive. This is not because the partial forms of co-operation that are emerging are a bad thing. Quite the reverse; they can yield exactly the sort of 'concrete achievements' that 'create *de facto* solidarity' to which Robert Schuman looked forward. The danger arises from the absence of any guiding principle governing their emergence, which means that in the end, as their importance to those involved increases, the Community could cease to be the central force of European co-operation and of the attempt to find forms of unity appropriate to the needs of the age.

It is essential therefore that ways should be found to enable partial forms of co-operation and projects involving only some member states to take place without threatening the essential unity of the whole. It must be recognized that it will be difficult to include some in ventures that are attractive to others because they have little to contribute. This would be the case, for example, with Ireland, Greece and Portugal in relation to aerospace and nuclear power. Another factor is that industrial projects set up to make a specific product, such as an aeroplane, can work effectively only on the basis of a limited number of partners. The more there are the more difficult the enterprise becomes to manage and the more costs tend to escalate. Finally it must be accepted that some member states simply will not wish to be involved in what others are doing; the most obvious example being security in respect of Ireland because of its neutrality, and probably Denmark and Greece as well.

These points are easy to make, but their consequences are not always easy to accommodate. If, for instance, a country is not involved in a European industrial project, it may well decide that it prefers to buy American, thereby reducing the market opportunities of the European product. In the case of an aeroplane that could be serious. Moreover, if it is for some reason excluded from a programme in which it wishes to be involved it may in turn refuse to participate in another where it is needed. If on the other hand it opts out of a particular area of activity, such as security, it may find that subjects in which it is interested are increasingly being dealt with under that heading rather than under those in which it is involved. In short, having everyone do everything at the same time may have proved unsatisfactory in recent years and be impossible in future, but the alternative is not a bed of roses either.

Europe therefore needs guiding principles and working methods of great flexibility. If the spirit of the Community is to be maintained every effort should be made to include all member states in what is being done. Sometimes this will involve simply leaving the door open so that outsiders may come in at a later date, as was done with the European Monetary System. On other occasions transitional periods, such as those that apply to new members and have been used several times for old ones on specific issues in recent years, will be the answer. Straightforward derogations from the Treaty that have to be renewed at stated intervals, such as those that France and others enjoy in respect of exchange controls, will also have a part to play.

When, for whatever reason, some member states have to be excluded from something that others are undertaking, they should be given a right to information and, if possible, even a financial stake. The Commission could be the instrument for this along the lines of its participation on behalf of the Community as a whole at World Economic Summits notwithstanding the participation of Britain, France, Germany and Italy as individuals in their own right. But in order to prevent 'free riding' such arrangements should not be expected to apply in the same way to those countries that opt out of spheres of activity of their own volition. It must also be accepted that the corollary of no member being forced to take part in a European policy is that no member should be able to prevent others from pursuing one.

Over time this will mean Europe developing in a fashion that resembles a core surrounded by a series of concentric circles. At the centre will lie the classical Community construction: the Common Market, the Common Agricultural Policy, the Common External Trade Policy, the Competition Policy plus the Social Fund, the Regional Fund, the Third World development policy and the other activities that have grown up around it. All member states, as at present, would have to participate fully in all of these, both because they interconnect and because they constitute the fruits of collective decisions taken over many years. In any case to attempt to unravel them now would open such a hornets' nest of arguments as to make work on any new ventures impossible. They will continue to expand and to be modernized, and will be added to as and when the member states agree to do so. Around them will radiate circles in which only some countries participate, the participants varying from one to another, though with a good deal of overlap, and a few countries involved in everything.

It is impossible at this stage to lay down hard and fast rules about how these different activities should be organized and managed. The European Monetary System and foreign policy co-ordination through Political Co-operation both show that the conventional Council machinery is very adaptable, and can encompass activities not laid down in the Treaty and not even fully involving all member states. Whenever possible it should be used for the sake of maintaining the maximum degree of coherence and consistency between different forms of co-operation. But this will not always be feasible.

In security matters, for instance, co-operation will often need to be carried into effect through the machinery of the North Atlantic Alliance, and will in any case need to be compatible with the requirements of that alliance. If this renders it unaccept-able to some member states, the European Council will in effect have to delegate work in that field to a body that includes only those wishing to be involved. This is one of the attractions of the Western European Union, since it already exists within the broad framework of the alliance, contains the seven Community members most interested in security and has its own secretariat which has had very little to do for many years. It could be constituted as it stands as a circle in its own right, if governments do not wish to establish any new arrangements, and could be expanded to take in other European countries, which would not necessarily have to be members of the Community. For their part industrial and research projects cannot be run efficiently by councils of ministers backed up by officials. They require their own corporate and management structures and, once the political decision to establish them has been taken, they need to be run on commercial and industrial rather than political lines.

Against such a varied background the Commission cannot expect to remain a universal executive arm. It will remain the central management agency for conventional Community activities and whatever is added to them. It will retain the right to put forward whatever ideas it feels appropriate across the whole spectrum of European co-operation, and it will be avail-able for whatever tasks the European Council lays upon it. It may represent the overall Community interest in activities involving only some member states. It should certainly retain its position as an independent honest broker, problem solver and trouble-shooter since a group of sovereign states trying to co-operate with each other will always require that. But in a variegated Europe its role will necessarily be more modest than was envisaged when a more uniform system was the objective.

It will not be the point at which everything that happens under Community auspices comes together. Suggestions have been made for establishing new secretariats to deal with Political Co-operation and to service the European Council. As this book goes to press the French are arguing that the Commission should not be involved with Eureka. The further development of the European Monetary System could one day lead to the establishment of a European version of the American Federal Reserve System. On the one hand the Community must avoid the proliferation and duplication of bureaucracies, and try whenever possible to use and adapt those that already exist. On the other it must be prepared to accept new ways of doing things as its range of activities evolves.

The point at which all the different strands of European co-operation come together should be the European Council. It is there that the action programme and guidelines for dealing with current problems to be followed by all member states should be laid down. It is there too that the final responsibility must rest for deciding on who participates in what, how the interests of the non-participants should be safeguarded and what arrangements should be made when the conventional Community institutions are not appropriate.

Its role should be symbolic as well as functional. While it is obvious that twelve countries cannot all take on the same commitments in the same manner as could be envisaged for six, it will not be easy to maintain an overall sense of unity within a more loosely organized structure. As a regular gathering of heads of state and government meeting on an equal footing and in turn in each other's countries to take decisions and exchange views, the European Council could become a common focus of attention throughout the Community. As such it would contribute to the creation of that sense of common purpose and shared interests transcending those of the individual member states that must lie at the heart of a successful European Union.

* * * 4 * * *

Journey to an Unknown Destination

Europe badly needs institutional and constitutional changes of the sort suggested in the preceding chapter. But too much should not be expected of them. They cannot achieve the impossible. As *Le Figaro* remarked after the referendum establishing the French Fifth Republic, 'Even an excellent constitution, which no country has, cannot suffice to reconcile different political points of view.'[1] That is even more the case when national interests are involved as well. A better institutional framework is a necessary, but not a sufficient, condition for enabling Europe to organize itself in a manner appropriate for the twenty-first century.

Another is understanding the scale of what is being attempted, and avoiding the temptation to trivialize it by speeches, proposals and pretences that take insufficient account of the immensity of the undertaking. Nothing like it has been seen before. Numerous attempts have been made in modern times to establish unity by force of arms over the area that now constitutes the Community. All have failed, even when directed by such a genius as Napoleon. The forces of nationalism, particularism and local loyalties, and the desire of most European people to run their own affairs proved too strong. Even the Hapsburg Empire with its remarkable capacity for survival was finally destroyed by the fissiparous forces of nationalism.

The Community represents a unique attempt on the part of people of different nationality with different historical experiences, most of whom have clashed destructively over the centuries, to live and work together and to find and pursue common objectives. When the United States was being formed its founding fathers were very conscious of the fact that they were creating something unlike any of the constitutional models and political systems then or previously in existence. The same is true of Europe today. The process is bound to be difficult and to take time. To say that there is no time and that it must be rushed is to fly in the face of experience. History is full of examples of political systems being cobbled together quickly only to wither or disintegrate in the course of a man's lifetime or that of his children. It teaches us that only those that put down roots and evolve in response to the needs of their participants flourish in the long run. Konrad Adenauer was right when he said: 'Europe is like a tree that grows; it cannot be fabricated.'[2] That is not to say that those responsible for it can sit back and let nature take its course. Far from it: the longer the process, the more essential it is for each generation of ministers and commissioners to contribute as much as it can without expecting to see dramatic results during one or two periods of office.

At this stage both patience and effort are particularly required. A tremendous ingathering of peoples has been carried through, but there is widespread uncertainty about what to do next. It is all a far cry from the days of Robert Schuman when Franco-German reconciliation within the framework of a peaceful unifying Europe was the objective and the European Coal and Steel Community followed by the European Economic Community were the means to attain it. To many the aim seemed visionary, and the means inadequate. But the enterprise was indubitably important and, thanks to the federalist and supranational idealism of the time, shot through with excitement. Now, by contrast, Europe has acquired the staid and unexciting quality that characterizes most ideas that have been in the public arena a long time.

There are, however, certain advantages about the present situation that should not be discounted. To begin with, the idea of European co-operation in general, and of the Community in particular, has proved it can work; imperfectly, certainly, with two steps back for every three forward, and in a manner fraught with frustration, disappointment and delay. But these phenomena are to be found in national capitals as well. Even the most long-established political systems can take decades to resolve big issues as well as others that are less big but arouse strong public passions. The length of time the position of trade unions in society has occupied the British political stage is one example of this, and the question of whether or not a third London airport should be located at Stansted is another. Moreover, although all governments and special interest groups may be relied upon to fight their corners in Europe for as long as they can, public opinion in most countries most of the time believes the Community ought to produce common solutions to common problems and common positions on external challenges. Inability to do so is widely regarded as failure while their achievement is hailed as success. Finally the need for European countries to work together in a common framework is accepted practically everywhere. The honeymoon era of the European idea may be over, but the mutual respect and habits of living and facing the world together that are essential to an enduring marriage have been established.

Guidelines

The purpose of this chapter is to lay down some ground rules for the further development of that union. It is not designed to be a manifesto, let alone a single general plan of the sort that the Schuman Declaration warned against, but which have been so common in recent years. It is rather intended to be a set of guidelines for the conduct of life. They do not lead ineluctably to some pre-ordained destination because it is no more possible to do that for states joined together in a common enterprise than for individuals. But they are put forward with the intention of facilitating the creation of the sort of 'concrete achievements' that will enable the states concerned to develop the political system of which they are all a part in whatever fashion and towards whatever end their people may wish.

Unrealistic expectations are a handicap in any marriage, and certainly in the Community – a word that itself serves to encourage them by conjuring up an image suggesting that disagreements and disputation must by definition be contrary to everything it stands for. In fact they are of its very essence. Nobody expects the President of the United States and the two Houses of Congress to cease their perpetual struggle and think of themselves as members of the same team. Their 'creative tension' is recognized as part of the process whereby decisions are taken, and regional as well as political differences reconciled. One of the principal purposes of a political system is to provide a framework within which the continuous struggle for power and influence among the interest groups, regions and factions contained within it may be conducted so that society does not break down and decisions may be taken. If it works well, it will over time help to generate and sustain a sense of common purpose and shared interests that transcends those of each of the parties involved. The same applies to the Community in conditions that are much more complex than those of a single country, however large. To suggest, as some political leaders do, that it can ever become a Utopia in which member states stop contesting with each other is to set a false standard, and one that the different regions of large federations do not live by.

Whatever institutional, or indeed constitutional, arrangements the Community adopts it will never be easy to reconcile positions and secure agreements. There will always be arguments, delays and deadlocks. Theatrical gestures – like the walkout by the Irish Prime Minister, Garret Fitzgerald, from the Brussels European Council in March 1984 in protest against plans to impose national quotas on milk production – must be expected as well. When political leaders representing real people and real interests are involved that is inevitable. National ministers must be seen, when necessary, to fight for their constituents. It is what they are elected to do, and it may be essential if they are to have any chance of reconciling those constituents to a compromise when one is finally reached.

The milk quotas against which Fitzgerald protested represented a massive problem for a country as dependent on its dairy industry as Ireland. He had to be seen to struggle. Arguments to the effect that the Community should be seen as a single market in which no distinction could be made between dairy farmers in Connemara, Frisia or Normandy flew in the face of political reality, and he could not be expected to accept such a line of reasoning, regardless of the purity of its Community doctrine. In the end, however, he had less difficulty than expected, and than Charles Haughey and the Fianna Fail opposition party hoped, in persuading his countrymen to accept the arrangement; they understood that he had done all in his power to safeguard Irish interests and probably obtained as many concessions as could have been secured.

They also recognized that Ireland benefits from the Community, and none more so than the farmers who on that occasion were losing out. This consideration is crucial. The fabric and cohesion of the individual member states are strong enough to withstand intense political divisions, and even fundamental structural changes. Their citizens recognize the right of governments to legislate, even on matters on which they themselves think it should not, and their loyalty to the state is rarely impaired by any antipathy they might feel to the government of the day.

The Community is in a different position. As the former French Socialist commissioner Edgard Pisani has said: 'It must constantly justify its existence by its actions; it can only exist if it renders some service to its members and to the international balance. If it performs those functions successfully, its existence will be unchallenged.'[3] If it does not, he might have added, it will ossify or fragment as the individual member states pursue their own interests and co-operate by other means. Like other international organizations, the Community is not so much an independent entity as a subsidiary jointly owned by others in order to achieve certain objectives. The scope and nature of those objectives will change, and their importance should increase over time. But as a subsidiary it must be able to convince its shareholders of its usefulness on a continuing basis. Its judges in that respect will be the governments and parliaments of the member states, the successors of those who called it into being in the first place.

So long as those governments and parliaments are convinced that the enterprise, taken as a whole, works in their interest and is consistent with their aspirations they will, depending on the political situation at home, be prepared to make compromises. But the more substantial their doubts on these basic points the more they will dig their heels in. That is why progress in the Community, and in looser forms of co-operation as well, generally has to be on the basis of package deals, which may be implicit and appreciated by only a handful of insiders rather than explicit, but are none the less trade-offs between advantages, actual or anticipated.

This is a point that all those who wish to achieve something at any given time would do well to remember, but that does not come easily to those schooled in British politics. In 1984 and the first half of 1985, while this book was being written, British ministers were hammering away on the need for progress in breaking down internal barriers to trade, an objective desirable in itself and laid down by the Treaty, but bound to cause difficulties in some member states. At the same time they adopted a dismissive attitude towards the European Monetary System, progress with which others had set their hearts on, and which must be both a condition and a consequence of the completion of the common internal market. A more sympathetic approach on the latter could only have strengthened their chances of success on the former. Ministers from countries in which coalitions have to be laboriously stitched together have less of a problem in this respect in the Community.

All governments, however, have difficulty in responding to each other's need to be able to demonstrate that the Community is working to their advantage, sometimes with dire results. In 1979 France and Germany were guilty of this fault when they tried to bully Mrs Thatcher into submission on the British budget problem instead of trying to defuse it before it got out of hand. In the early 1980s some of the smaller richer countries that were receiving large gains from the Community budget made a similar error by failing to offer Germany an abatement of its open-ended commitment, thereby helping to harden German attitudes on other matters.

The attitude of member state governments and parliaments is also a reason why the Commission must avoid giving the impression of trying to encroach on the prerogatives of member states, and of wishing ultimately to see the Community institutions supplant them. According to federalist ambitions and rhetoric that is, of course, precisely what should happen, but in practice governments, supported by parliaments, will invariably oppose anything that smacks of a transfer of sovereignty. That applies as much to those who subscribe to federalist rhetoric as to those who do not.

An illustration of this is provided by what happened in 1983 when the Commission proposed that the power to increase the Community's financial 'own resources' should be transferred from national parliaments to the Council of Ministers and the European Parliament acting together. Much was currently being said about the need to increase the powers of the European Parliament, and to give it rights of co-decision with the Council of Ministers. Here, if ever there was one, was a practical proposal to do exactly that, as distinct from the more theoretical formulas that are generally put forward. The German Foreign Minister, Hans-Dietrich Genscher, the author along with Italian Foreign Minister Emilio Colombo of a recent declaration on European Union, listened attentively as the scheme was outlined in the Council. He then said that he disagreed, and that he did so *inter alia* as a member of the Bundestag who did not wish to see that body lose such a power to the Community institutions. The proposal died at that moment.

Genscher took the lead because, as the biggest contributor to the Community budget, Germany's interests were directly at risk. A suggestion to give a European Monetary Fund authority over the central banks of the member states, including the Bundesbank, in the context of the further development of the European Monetary System, could meet a similar fate because of German fears that it would lead to their importing the 'lax' monetary habits of their neighbours, and will require the most careful preparation and sensitivity to their preoccupations in order to succeed. Other governments with a different range of interests and attitudes would take a different position from the Germans on those two points, but be equally negative in relation to others and require equally careful handling in order to overcome their doubts.

National governments will always look closely at whatever the Commission proposes in order to ensure that it does not infringe their prerogatives. They will also invariably need convincing that it is in their own interest, or can be adapted to be so, before being prepared to consider it seriously. Powerful arguments of a practical nature will be required to convince them that something can be better done collectively or on a centralized basis – which are not necessarily the same – rather than individually. These are facts of life that, however far from the theory of the Community they may be, are most unlikely to alter in the foreseeable future. Consequently the Commission and others seeking to promote European policies must take them into account.

In this connection perhaps Europe has something to learn from the Swiss. Lord Bryce once said that 'the prosaic and humdrum character of Swiss political life' does not invite contemplation,[4] and one can see what he means. None the less the Swiss succeed, despite being divided on linguistic and religious grounds – either one of which, as Belgian and Irish experience shows, can cause immense difficulties – in living together in what is indubitably an entity with a common purpose and shared interests that transcend those of its component parts. Over the years, and in a gradual fashion, they have also transferred a number of powers and functions from the cantons to the federal level as circumstances demanded.

This is partly because the Swiss are sensible people who can grasp the logic of events, so long as they are not required to do so too quickly. But another essential element in the peaceful and gradual evolution of their political system is that the burden of proof has always lain with the centralizers. It is they who have to show that a useful purpose would be served by an increase in the powers and responsibilities of the central administration. This is no formal matter, as the preamble to the constitution explicitly states that one of the purposes of that constitution is to guarantee the continued existence of the cantons. Consequently a functional case must be made out to show that the cantons and their people will be better off as a result of the centre gaining powers and responsibilities, whether they be at the expense of the cantons or new ones that the cantons cannot adequately discharge.

If that point needs to be spelt out in the circumstances of Switzerland, a confederation that has evolved over hundreds of years but in which the canton rather than the confederation remains most people's principal focus of loyalty, how much more it needs emphasizing in the context of the Community. I made this point once to a former Dutch Foreign Minister, who had been involved in the Community's early days. 'I cannot accept it,' he replied. 'You are thinking in too pragmatic and utilitarian a fashion. Switzerland is a marriage of convenience. Europe was inspired by emotion.' Without that emotion Community Europe would not have established itself, and it remains important, which is why practical measures need to be sustained and promoted by appropriate forms of rhetoric. But in contemporary Europe emotion and appeals to the ideals and models that provided inspiration in the 1950s and 1960s will not by themselves achieve much, though they can still generate applause.

If governments, parliaments and people are to be persuaded really to co-operate in a European context, they must be convinced that the co-operation is complementary to what they are trying to do themselves and adds to it, not that the European dimension replaces the national one. Europe must aim to enhance the scope and capacity of the individual nation states, not to take over from them. In these circumstances, supranational ambitions can be the enemy of practical unity, while a recognition of national realities is the best way to achieve it. That is the paradox that lies at the heart of what is sometimes called 'the Construction of Europe'.

The chances of deepening that co-operation and extending the range and number of common ventures and common policies will be enhanced if the Community can discipline itself so that only a limited number of specific objectives are being pursued at any one time. This does not mean that the objectives themselves should be modest, nor that the participants should not envisage them as initial steps on a long road to more ambitious forms of joint endeavour. Quite the contrary. What it does mean is that the Community must not bite off more than it can chew only to find itself incapacitated by indigestion.

To function effectively it must recognize that the complexity of its functions, like those of any other human activity, increases exponentially with the number of objectives being pursued and the number of players involved. As the number of players is predetermined it is essential that the number of objectives be kept under tight control. The more there are being pursued simultaneously, the greater the number of detailed policies, programmes, project managements and consultative procedures that will be required, and the more cumbersome the Community will become. The nature and scope of the coalition programme outlined in the previous chapter must therefore be chosen with great care. In addition, its component parts, taken together, must correspond with the real interests of the countries concerned and be as invulnerable as possible to the vagaries wrought by changes of government, since if such changes lead to attempts to alter significantly the balance or content of the programme it could easily unravel.

These principles are, as is so often the case, easier to enunciate than to live by. Even when relatively like-minded governments are in power in a majority of member states, the range of differences between their underlying situations and domestic priorities is considerable. It is necessary only to compare such basic economic statistics as their respective inflation rates and public deficits, let alone the variety of their social structures and underlying hopes and aspirations, to appreciate that. Accordingly whenever ministers meet, and this is perhaps particularly true of Presidents and Prime Ministers, there is a perennial temptation to adopt too many targets in a vain attempt to provide something for everyone.

The image of a children's party in which the games have to be carefully planned so that there is at least one in which each of those invited may shine comes irresistibly to mind. Nor is it an inappropriate comparison. If heads of government are to secure support at home for European objectives that are not high among their own national and party priorities and which, regardless of the benefits they may bring, will cause domestic difficulties, they must show that the coalition programme includes other more attractive items as well. To strike a balance between not trying to do too much on the one hand and the need to secure a reasonable balance between the interests of the various governments involved on the other can never be easy. It is rendered more difficult in the Community by the inflationary pressure exerted by the demands of the European Parliament, the Commission's attempts to satisfy them and that body's own tendency, like most bureaucracies, to assess its own virility in terms of the number of proposals it produces.

Another complication in attempting to limit the number of priorities to be pursued simultaneously stems from the fact that policies are rarely self-contained. They spill over into fields other than those for which they were originally intended. Thus moves to create a real common market are bound to involve action on a variety of other subjects that at first sight might seem to bear little relation to it. The environment is one since, to take an example, if more than one emission standard for car exhausts is introduced, the effect could be to fragment the already imperfect common market in motor cars. There are also bound to be consequences for the way in which such matters as drugs and firearms are regulated and policed.

While the need to meet the political requirements of different governments plus what might be termed knock-on effects make it hard to limit the number of specific objectives being pursued at any one time, there is another principle that should be brought to bear which works in the opposite direction. It is that all policy proposals should be judged according to whether they would in practice unite or disunite the countries involved. Unity should be regarded not simply as an aim, but also as a test. The member states should try to ensure that whatever they set out to do collectively has the effect of binding them together rather than of driving them apart.

The establishment of a common internal market passes this

test since it would not only help to integrate the economies of the member states, it would also enable their citizens to travel, settle and work wheresoever they pleased. By contrast an attempt to harmonize the constitutions of the different member states would set people at each other's throats. The acceptance by all member states of each other's professional and academic qualifications would be unifying, but an attempt to harmonize their education systems would be the reverse. The same applies to the encouragement of language teaching on the one hand, and any attempt to undermine the position of minority languages on the other.

Similar distinctions may be drawn in determining how policies that are conducted at the European level should be implemented. The creation of a really common internal market, to continue with that example, requires that lorries should no longer be stopped at frontiers so that V A T may be collected, but this does not mean that each country should be required to levy the tax at identical rates, any more than that the states of the United States should be required to introduce uniform rates of sales tax. The main need is for watertight arrangements to be made for its subsequent collection from the importer. By the same token the encouragement of companies to extend their activities beyond frontiers no more demands a common company statute than in the United States, where each state has its own. Accounting and disclosure standards need to be brought more into line and made more transparent, and taxation obstacles should be removed. But such questions as whether to have single-tier or two-tier boards or whether to encourage worker participation should be left to the individual countries.

In deciding both what should be attempted at the European level and how to set about it, those concerned should bear in mind these words of the then President of the European Court,

Josse Mertens de Wilmars, at the twenty-fifth anniversary celebrations: 'At the beginning of this century, Paul Valéry urged us, as if by premonition, rather to differ in unity than to be similar in disunity.' Napoleon's exhortation in his memoirs against 'tormenting the people with trivia'* might be borne in mind as well. Too often in the past the Commission and the European Parliament have sought standardization for its own sake and become too much devoted to the regulation of detail.

As was stated above, the purpose of this chapter is to lay down ground rules, not to draw up a manifesto, the contents and balance of which are bound to need adjustment with the passage of time. It is, however, necessary briefly to outline the type and mix of subjects that should at present be accorded priority in order to indicate how the broad principles would translate into action, and the fields in which the Community should be seeking to create more of Schuman's 'concrete achievements'.

Policies – Internal

The first point to be made in this context is that the Community does not start with a clean slate. Much as many would like to avert their gaze from the stale and intractable problems of the past in order to concentrate on planning their route through the sunny uplands of the future, that cannot be done. The capacity and moral authority that the Community brings to

---

*The context in which this was written is perhaps less helpful to my case since Napoleon was inveighing against those scientists responsible for standardizing weights and measures by means of the metric system. He thought it would be a 'source of difficulties for several generations', whereas in fact it has turned out to be extremely useful.

new issues are inevitably affected by its record on those with which it is already concerned. That is why the reform of the Common Agricultural Policy, one of the foundation stones on which the whole edifice is built, must feature high on any serious list of priorities. The arrival of Spain and Portugal makes this more urgent than ever. Although they will increase the Community's internal demand for surplus temperate food-stuffs, such as meat and milk products from the northern countries, their potential for increasing the Community's total output of Mediterranean products could turn out to be very expensive.

The CAP's faults are not unique; surpluses and extravagant costs have for many years characterized the agricultural policies of the United States, Switzerland and Japan to name only three. Its successes in providing for the orderly run-down of the numbers of people engaged in agriculture in the 1960s and 1970s and in maintaining balanced rural populations in many parts of Europe today should not be discounted. Nor should the political and social problems inherent in bringing more stringent economic criteria to bear be underestimated. The German resist-ance to the Commission's attempts in 1985 to cut cereal prices illustrates that most dramatically, but so, to a lesser extent, does the hostile reaction in Britain, despite its small rural population and strong views in favour of curbing agricultural expenditure, to the imposition of milk quotas in 1984. The CAP's contribution to the remarkable improvement in the efficiency of European agriculture over the years should also be appreciated. If those sectors of industry that have benefited from large subsidies and state support had all used their bounty equally well, it would be a cause for rejoicing.

None the less when all these points have been taken into account the fact remains that the irresponsibility of so many decisions taken in the agricultural field, the costs and surpluses to which they have given rise, the refusal for so long to face up to their consequences and the sourness and disillusion with the European idea that have resulted now weigh on the Community like a failed exam as it turns to face the future. Until the CAP's well-known problems have been brought under control the Community is, in practice, most unlikely to be entrusted with the responsibility for any further substantial expenditure programme. The key to the resolution of these problems lies in the capitals of the member states, and above all in some of those that call most insistently for the further development of the Community. Whatever criticisms may be levelled at the adequacy or otherwise of the Commission's proposals in recent years, it has been the refusal of governments in the Council of Ministers to limit output and restrain costs that has created the present situation.

Drastic action is now required. The most straightforward would be to reduce the guaranteed prices that underpin the market to levels much nearer those prevailing on world markets. But on the basis of experience I find it impossible to imagine the circumstances in which agreement could be reached on such a programme. A mix will therefore be required between action on prices and the imposition of quotas on producers. In addition the availability of funds from the Community budget to subsidize exports must be cut back. On the other side of the balance sheet, income aids will need to be paid to some of the smaller and poorer farmers – for whom there is no alternative employment – both for social reasons and to prevent a depopulation of the countryside. These will have to be administered according to Community rules to prevent one country's farmers from deriving advantages at the expense of another's, but in many cases there is no reason why these should not be paid for out of national funds rather than the Community budget.

By themselves Agriculture Ministers will never be able to agree on such a package. Accordingly it is necessary that their deliberations should be subjected to the same sort of budgetary discipline as applies to spending programmes within the individual member states, and as they would be subjected to in most Community countries if they were administered on a national rather than a European basis. This in turn means that the Agriculture Ministers must be required to work within guidelines laid down by the Finance Ministers and backed up by the European Council. The longer the present state of affairs continues, the more corrosive to unity it will become, and the greater the problems it will generate with the United States and the Community's other trading partners. The sooner it can be tackled the more capable the Community will be to respond to other challenges.

The completion of the common internal market has been on the Community agenda for even longer than the reform of the CAP, but has recently acquired a new aura of excitement and immediacy. The creation of a single market of 320 million people, significantly larger in population terms even than that of the United States, has the scale and grandeur of a major political objective. At a time of mounting concern over Europe's capacity to keep up with the United States, Japan and other newly industrialized countries, it is in keeping with the spirit of the times. The idea that Europe needs an industrial base and a home market for its goods and services comparable with those of its main competitors is readily appreciated, as is the fact that the means to provide them lie ready to hand in the Treaty of Rome. Their creation is by no means all that is needed, but given the particular responsibilities vested in the Community and the terms of the Treaty, it is what the Community as such should concentrate on.

Such a market cannot, of course, guarantee success to any individual company or industry. Only their own efforts in management, production, sales and research can do that. But the larger their domestic market the greater the prizes to be won by the most successful competitors within it, and the more able they will then be to hold their own against the Americans, Japanese and others both at home and overseas. This is true not only of large companies with long production runs that need mass markets. It applies equally to small companies that supply and service them, and to those small companies with specialist, high-value-added products for which a national market is not adequate to sustain profitable production in the long run. In addition the larger the prospective opportunities for manufacturing and service industries, the more those who provide capital can be persuaded to take risks.

European industry and commerce need to be given, as far as possible, the same opportunities in their home market as those enjoyed by the Americans in theirs. That requires a dramatic reduction in frontier formalities and the creation of a situation in which goods and services that are allowed on to the market in one member state should, so long as they meet certain basic 'Euro'-requirements, automatically be eligible for sale in all others, instead of having to comply with differing health, safety, technical and other standards as at present. It also requires governments themselves to open up their own procurement programmes – which, as described in Chapter 1, account for between 7 and 10 per cent of the Community's total domestic product and are almost entirely confined to national suppliers. The aim should be to create a situation in which managements can consider the Community as a single market in which they take their decisions on the basis of economic efficiency rather than having constantly to try to maximize the benefits and minimize the disadvantages arising from the continued existence of separate national markets.

Its achievement will be a difficult and thankless task in political terms, both for the Commission in making specific proposals and for the governments that have to carry them into effect. In every country any domestic interest that feels threatened will seek to rouse its political representatives and public opinion against what is being attempted, and experience shows that public opinion is generally more immediately responsive to carefully orchestrated producer lobbies than to proposals that, by opening the way for more foreign competition, widen consumer choice and lead on to lower prices. Proposals designed to prevent hidden obstacles to free trade will be ridiculed as 'Brussels brainstorms', and opposed as needless interference in domestic affairs. Progress will not be made in the sort of dramatic leaps and bounds that attract favourable publicity, but through the undramatic pursuit of what will often appear boring and minor issues. Only if the European Council is prepared to lay down specific objectives, backed if necessary by deadlines, and only if deadlocks can, after all else fails, be broken by majority votes, will it be achieved.

The creation of a large domestic European market would not only serve to release the energies of European companies and facilitate their expansion into what are now distinct national markets. It would also help to harness the inventiveness and experience of American and Japanese companies to Europe's development. If Europe is to catch up in those areas in which it lags behind, and if it is to derive the maximum benefit from those in which it is fully competitive, it cannot do so only through its own efforts. There are a number of European companies – probably more than is generally supposed – that have shown they can compete successfully against all comers not just within Europe, but in the United States and elsewhere. Other European companies, however, would stand to gain from alliances with the Americans and Japanese that give them access to those companies' experience, research and, if possible, markets in return for advantages in Europe. This is the philosophy that has inspired the Italian Olivetti, for instance, in its link-ups with American Telephone & Telegraph on the one hand and the Japanese Toshiba on the other. The more fragmented the European market the harder it is for European companies to negotiate such alliances on the most advantageous terms, whereas the greater the opportunities they can offer the more beneficial those alliances will be.

Olivetti's are more ambitious than most, but many other European companies have followed the same route. In May 1984 Carlo de Benedetti, the group's chairman, estimated that out of 200 joint venture agreements by European companies in the electronics industry in the previous year 50 per cent involved American partners and 30 per cent Japanese, while only 18 per cent were between Europeans themselves.[5] Yet the concept of external alliances continues to arouse suspicion and disapproval in some circles. The emphasis, it is argued, should be on co-operation between European companies, and the impression is sometimes given that arrangements between Europeans and non-Europeans are politically second best and possibly undesirable as well. That is a mistaken approach. The Olivetti arrangement has much to contribute in terms of opening up new horizons for the European economy, and each individual deal should be judged on its own merits.

When European companies expand into each other's countries they can be expected to employ a variety of methods, such as direct sales, take-overs and the establishment of subsidiaries as well as joint ventures and partnerships, and often a combination of two or more. Joint ventures and partnerships are notoriously difficult to organize compared with businesses with a single boss, and their prospective advantages outweigh their disadvantages only if each partner has specific contributions to make and specific objectives in view. That typically is the case where one is gaining access to a new market, whether Europe or the United States, and the other access to new technology, or where a swap involving both elements is concerned. For this reason such arrangements can be expected to occur relatively frequently between European and non-European companies, whereas within a real common internal market European companies themselves should increasingly feel able to expand across frontiers without recourse to them. In the case of government-sponsored programmes involving more than one government they will obviously have a prominent role to play, but in the purely private sector other methods are likely to prove more popular.

The creation of a real common internal market is the biggest single contribution that the Community as such could make towards the restoration of Europe's industrial competitiveness. It would provide the private sector with both a framework and a launching pad that cannot be secured in any other way. It also provides a classic example of how Europe can enhance the scope and capacity of what can be achieved at national level. But it is not the only action required within the European context.

One of the clichés of European gatherings at any level is that the total research expenditure of the European countries as separate entities is greater than that of the United States or Japan, yet they get back less than either from their investment. An illustration of this may be found in telecommunications where the British government estimated in early 1984 that European companies had spent $10 billion developing ten different digital switching systems, while three American companies had spent $3 billion and two Japanese firms $1.5 billion.[6] Similar examples can be found in a host of other industries. In these circumstances the case for European governments to seek ways of jointly mobilizing and harnessing their national efforts in certain high-technology and capital-intensive industrial fields is very strong.

As is also pointed out at these gatherings and in many books and articles, the United States has derived enormous benefits across the whole range of its industrial life from its defence and space programmes, and may be expected to reap another massive harvest of industrial and technological progress from the Strategic Defence Initiative. By themselves European countries cannot mount anything remotely similar. If they are to offer their indigenous industrial and scientific communities opportunities that are in any degree comparable they can only hope to do so on a collective basis. At a more modest level they also need to build on such successes as Airbus and Ariane and extend them into other fields. On both fronts even the Community provides an inadequate base which needs the reinforcement that can be provided by companies from other European countries. These countries have indeed for long been represented in Ariane and the Joint European Torus nuclear fusion project, to name two examples. The significance of their contribution was emphasized in the most unmistakable terms when agreement was announced in June 1985 between the French state-controlled defence and electronics group Matra and Norsk Data of Norway to develop a computer in what was hailed as the first project to get under way in the French-sponsored Eureka scheme.

If the 'concrete achievements' that the people of all European countries need in the industrial sector are to be created, there is one lesson from the past that must not be forgotten. Bearing in mind the experience of the Common Agricultural Policy, it is essential that any attempt to organize an overall Common Industrial Policy should be avoided. What Europe needs are specific programmes and projects with limited, explicit and mutually compatible objectives designed to create what the Schuman Declaration called '*de facto* solidarity', not general plans that promise the earth and end in a mad scramble for the European pork-barrel.

The point about objectives is crucial. There is always a danger in European affairs that political, industrial, scientific and even defence lobbies will invoke 'Europe' as a sort of trump card to secure approval for projects that would not go ahead on their merits, or as a reason for their particular country entering one that might promise generous returns to the special interest group pressing for it while not being in the interest of the country concerned as a whole. The principle of regarding unity not simply as an aim but also as a test applies with special force in the industrial arena. General Jacques Mitterrand, the President's brother and former chairman of Aerospatiale, has pointed out that in collaborative projects 'nothing can be done unless the fundamental interests of the participants are preserved'.[7] It is important not to forget that, nor the equally important point that ventures embarked upon primarily for so-called political reasons are more likely to end in discord and disarray than those based on sound industrial, commercial and research criteria and run on equally sound financial lines. It is up to those who have to take the political decisions without which nothing involving governments can happen to ensure that these considerations are given their due weight.

This will mean on occasion that more than one line of

development is taking place in the same field in Europe at the same time. Far from being a misfortune, that can be desirable. One of the mistakes that those who wish to see a more co-ordinated and organized European industrial and research effort frequently make is to assume that there must invariably be a single European 'champion'. But the fact that there is too much overlapping and duplicated industrial research and development going on in Europe at present does not mean that it would be right to move to the opposite extreme. It is almost always better to have some competition than none. Obviously there can be room for only one United States space programme or Strategic Defence Initiative, and the same applies to any European counterpart, but that restriction should not apply to projects designed to result in a specific product. It is impossible for governments, or even industrialists and scientists, to know in advance which of several possible approaches will yield the best result. For as long as the money, talent and willingness to try more than one are available in Europe, the more likely it is that real champions capable of competing on equal terms anywhere in the world will emerge at the end of the day. Moreover, if some of them have Americans, Japanese and other outsiders among their participants that should be regarded as a sensible way of harnessing the talents of the rest of the world to Europe's benefit, rather than a point of criticism.

The establishment of a real common market and of more far-reaching forms of industrial co-operation should be matched and reinforced by an intensification of efforts to co-ordinate economic policy. 'Co-ordination' is the appropriate word rather than something stronger. Raymond Barre, with his unique experience as a former French Prime Minister and Vice-President of the Commission, has argued in relation to both wider forms of international co-operation and the European Community:

'They have not thus far created effective obligations for governments. Each country is ready to consider the wishes expressed by its partners or by international organizations or to listen to very discreet advice from them. None the less, in practice each country vigilantly safeguards its freedom of action in making economic policy.'[8] This is a realistic assessment. The key decisions on fiscal, monetary and exchange rate policies are widely regarded as being among the 'crown jewels' of national sovereignty. They also constitute one of the principal areas of domestic policy debate, and may at any time become central issues in election campaigns or the events leading to a change of coalition partners. Accordingly no government can bind its successors, or be expected to hand over final responsibility in these matters to outside bodies.

Recognition of this fundamental fact of contemporary political life, and with it the equally fundamental consequence, in Barre's words, that 'therefore it behoves each country to solve its problems by its own efforts', should not be used as excuses for doing nothing. The interdependence of European economies is such that it must be in the interests of all to ensure that each government pays as much attention as possible to the needs and interests of its partners when taking its own economic decisions. This is also an essential prerequisite for any effective combined European initiative in relation to United States economic and monetary policy.

The aim should be to build up habits of consultation and cooperation between member states that public opinion in each comes to regard as normal and useful, to the point that any new administration will feel bound to continue them, whatever changes of emphasis in its own national approach it might wish to make. George Vest, one of the wisest of United States ambassadors to the European Community, has described 'the habit of co-operation as one of the strongest bonds between the member states and one of the hardest for outsiders to assess'. In economic policy it provides the only enduring basis on which to build.

The procedures of the European Monetary System have already demonstrated their worth in this respect. In part this is because of the continuous process of consultation to which they give rise at the ministerial, official and central bank levels. All member states – including Britain and Greece, which until the arrival of Spain and Portugal were the only member states not in the system's exchange rate mechanism – have participated in and benefited from that. But it is the mechanism which is crucial because of the way it has led to parity changes being conducted through negotiation, rather than unilateral action so that the strong currencies go up while the weak go down; and both sets of countries undertake the economic measures judged necessary to sustain the new rates.

It is on this experience that the Community should continue to build by undertaking a number of practical initiatives designed to increase the system's scope for effective action. The most long-awaited and in political terms the most important is the entry of Britain into the exchange rate mechanism. For their part France, Italy, Belgium, Ireland and Denmark should dismantle their remaining, and in some cases substantial, exchange control regulations. The effectiveness of the consultation procedures should be further enhanced by governments not simply committing themselves to prior discussion of macro-economic decisions, but promising in advance to forgo measures that would disrupt their partners, such as the import deposit scheme introduced by the Italians a few years ago, without the Community's prior agreement. The co-ordination of the central banks' interventions on world currency markets, notably in relation to the dollar, and their borrowing policies should also be still further increased, both in normal circumstances and at times of crisis.

Desirable as these developments would be in helping to integrate still further the economies of the member states, they would, for the most part, be understood only by the *cognoscenti* actually involved in managing or monitoring economic policy. They would have little impact on the public at large. Yet if habits of co-operation are to secure the degree of public acceptance that would in practice bind governments they need some form of outward manifestation that the public can grasp.

Table 5 Composition of the ECU

	%
W. German mark	32.5
French franc	19.4
British pound	14.9
Dutch florin	10.3
Italian lira	9.4
Belgian franc	8.3
Danish krone	2.7
Greek drachma	1.0
Irish pound	1.2
Luxembourg franc	0.3

* On the basis of 8 October 1985 exchange rate.

That should be provided by the ECU, the EMS's most spectacular achievement to date. This currency unit, made up of fixed amounts of ten Community currencies, already performs many of the functions of ordinary money. As was pointed out in Chapter 1, it became third only to the dollar and the Deutschmark in terms of international bond issues in 1983. The Community budget is drawn up in ECUs, and within the EMS governments use them to settle some of their accounts with each other. The value of each individual currency within the EMS is defined in terms of certain quantities of ECU, and it is in a limited way a reserve asset since all central banks including the Bank of England deposit with the European Monetary Co-operation Fund the equivalent of 20 per cent of their gold and foreign exchange resources. Some companies use ECUs for internal accounting purposes and for external invoicing, and in most countries, including Britain, individuals can open ECU accounts with their banks.

Governments made this possible by the original act of creation, and in most cases they have contributed their subsequent encouragement as well. But the most impressive progress has been made by markets, and the organizations and individuals that make them up, developing the ECU in response to their own needs and for specific financial and commercial purposes. It has also been secured despite Germany, unlike others, refusing to accept the ECU as a foreign currency. A combination of official and unofficial action will continue to be needed in future. Natural growth in response to market needs should remain a principal avenue of advance, but the role of governments in making that possible will be crucial, and if really ambitious targets are to be achieved the German authorities must come into line with their partners.

The establishment of such targets would do more than anything else to give credibility to the Community's efforts to co-ordinate economic policy, and to give concrete expression to the words 'European Economic Community'. Externally the aim should be to establish the ECU as an alternative international currency to the dollar in which countries, whether members of the Community or not, would be prepared to hold reserves and in which widely traded commodities such as oil could be priced. Internally it should be to create a form of parallel currency for use in appropriate circumstances alongside those of the member states. The ECU's use by governments for settling accounts could extend to companies and to individuals for cross-frontier bills, for which traveller's cheques and credit cards are already being introduced. If, in addition to these functions, the ECU could be given physical form in the shape of a coin to circulate in all member states, that would provide both a practical and a symbolic means of establishing its status. This programme will take a long time to achieve and will in due course require the creation of some form of European central bank, which is worth pursuing both because of the contribution it would make to unifying the European economy and because the world needs a new international currency to take its place alongside the dollar.

Policies – External

The Community's pursuit of greater internal unity and coherence needs to be matched by a more united response to external events and challenges. This is necessary in order to enable the member states to make their voice heard and their influence felt, as much in the capital of their great ally the United States as in other less friendly and potentially more hostile parts of the world. It is equally vital for internal reasons since foreign policy divisions can have a very damaging impact on the whole fabric of the Community and on the perception of people in the member states towards each other. It is necessary only to consider what the reaction of the Germans would be if the Federal Republic's response to a crisis in East Germany differed substantially from that of its allies, or how the British would have reacted if their partners had not rallied round during the Falklands episode, to appreciate this.

At first sight it seems absurd that the members of the Community should not be able to get their act together and present a united front to the world. The danger of Europe becoming, as Jung warned in 1930, 'a mere hyphen between America and Asia' seems so evident. But attitudes to foreign affairs are formed as much by history, temperament and prejudice as by political debate or rational assessments of where the national interest lies. Sometimes this can be helpful, as with the French and German determination to put the past behind them. On other occasions it can be a constant source of danger, as with Greece's hereditary obsession with Turkey. The links with other parts of the world brought to the Community by some member states enrich it and widen its horizons, but they too can be a complicating factor as would certainly have been the case with the Falklands if Spain had been a member at that time.

Political Co-operation, the Community's process of foreign policy co-ordination, reflects these realities. It works exclusively on the basis of consensus, and no one has ever suggested that majority votes should be employed. This means that if one of the Twelve objects to a proposal no Community decision can be taken by the other eleven. They are left to take their own on a national basis. There are, however, some powerful factors tending towards unity, or at least silent acquiescence by a dissentient minority. The constant exchange of confidential diplomatic information between the member states and the frequency with which their ministers and officials meet help to create a common view. The desire of most to promote, whenever possible, a common position and the moral pressure this creates is another. So too, as the Greek support for Britain over the Falklands shows, is the realization that a precedent created on one occasion for one member state may be helpful in analogous circumstances to another. The combined effect of these influences should not be underestimated. When Douglas Hurd returned to the Foreign and Commonwealth Office as a minister of state in 1979 he found, even then, that they constituted 'the biggest change in diplomatic method' since he first entered the department as a young diplomat in 1952.[9]

The ideas put forward at the Milan European Council in June 1985 for formalizing the previously informal consultations between governments and binding them to consult before launching individual foreign policy initiatives, and for establishing a small secretariat to assist in this, provide a realistic means of building on what has been achieved. As with the procedures of the European Monetary System, they have the potential over time of deepening George Vest's 'habit of co-operation' to the point where it becomes accepted by public opinion and governments alike as the normal framework within which member states conduct their foreign relations. That in turn should help to avoid the chaos and prevarication that attended the Community's response to the Polish crisis in December 1981 and the shooting down of the Korean airliner in September 1983, described in Chapter 2, besides encouraging a united Community approach to ongoing international negotiations and problems.

It is to be hoped, however, that the new procedures are not put to a severe test too soon. In the light of member states' very different histories and views of the world, the time required for the 'habit of co-operation' to be transformed into co-ordinated action on a regular and continuous basis is likely to be greater in foreign affairs than is often realized. There will continue to be occasions on which a united front is not possible with only some member states able to pursue the same line together. In those circumstances it will be important to try to ensure that the dissentients stand aside rather than mount a rival operation. What has already been achieved may be likened to islands of co-operation in a sea of non-co-operation. The aim must be to make those islands ever greater while reducing the weight of water and corrosive potential of the salt in the remaining pools of non-co-operation.

As with the EMS, other measures that can be appreciated by the general public as well as by the *cognoscenti* are also required to strengthen the bonds between the people of the member states themselves. One that would help to achieve that and serve a useful purpose as well would be the establishment of joint diplomatic missions in third countries. For many reasons, including trade promotion, individual member states will wish to maintain their own embassies in important capitals. But the cost and manpower demands of running a world-wide network is already too much for some smaller ones, and even the larger cannot afford a presence in every African, Asian and Latin American capital. The big ones are also running down their consular facilities in many important provincial cities in major countries because of the cost of maintaining them. In all these centres member states could pool their resources and arrange to be represented on a joint basis. To lay down hard and fast rules on such matters would be wrong because the spread of interests of the member states varies too much; a country or capital that one would regard as unimportant could be significant for another. What is required is for member states to get into the habit of having embassies and consulates in common in those places where it suits them. Sometimes such missions might be on behalf of only two or three member states; sometimes on behalf of six or seven or even all twelve. As experience of this way of working together increases so their number could be expected to grow.

One purpose of this proposal is to heighten the awareness citizens of member states have of their membership of a common enterprise. But the extent to which it would heighten the outside world's perception of the Community as an entity in its own right should not be underestimated. Already it is customary when a commissioner arrives on an official visit in a non-Community country in which the Commission itself has no office for the ambassador of the country holding the presidency of the Council of Ministers to welcome him at the airport just as a national ambassador welcomes a national minister. Accordingly when I arrived in Kuala Lumpur in 1983 to represent the Community at the conference with ASEAN, referred to in Chapter 2, the German ambassador was there to greet me. At that time Anglo-Malaysian relations were going through a period of some strain, and the Malaysians were both surprised and impressed by this visible evidence of the extent to which the Community countries are part of a common enterprise.

Another initiative that would emphasize the common approach of Community countries to events in other parts of the world would be a strengthening of their common aid programme. This would be particularly so in the case of famine and disaster relief in which no special European national interests are involved, such as where the recipient country orders the capital goods to be purchased with the aid money it receives. The means to provide assistance are furnished in part by the CAP, and the sole object is to get the food, medical supplies and other equipment that are needed, as well as specialist help, to the stricken areas as quickly as possible. By themselves European countries lack the capacity of the Americans in this field. Together they can do more than would be possible as individuals.

The combination of closer foreign policy co-operation, the creation of a real common market and more industrial co-operation is bound to draw the countries concerned deeper into the field of security and defence. In the modern world it is impossible to mark a clear line between civilian and military activities. That is true of both industry and diplomacy. As the United States space and defence programmes have repeatedly demonstrated, and as the Strategic Defence Initiative no doubt will, developments in micro-electronics, telecommunications and a host of other industries have both military and civil applications, and the companies involved are often the same in both. If government procurement programmes are to be opened up in one area, it is difficult to see how they could remain firmly closed in the other. Similarly it is not necessary to subscribe to Clausewitz's view that 'war is nothing but the continuation of politics with the admixture of other means' to appreciate that it is hardly possible to engage in serious foreign policy co-ordination without considering its security implications. At the end of the day the relationships between most European countries on the one hand and, in their opposite ways, the United States and the Soviet Union on the other are dominated by considerations of defence and security.

There are other factors to be taken into account as well. All European countries are deeply concerned about the rising cost of all forms of defence procurement; and many are worried by the degree to which they are dependent in this respect upon purchases from the United States, with the implications that has for the competitiveness of their own industries against the Americans in the non-defence sectors. In recent years there has been a ten-to-one imbalance in transatlantic trade in defence equipment in favour of the United States. The lessons are clear. Unless European countries are able to pool their resources to a greater degree it will be impossible for them either to afford all the equipment they feel they need or to maintain the industrial capability on this side of the Atlantic to provide it. Because of the link between civil and military uses in so many fields this would have dire consequences for Europe's continued industrial competitiveness. There is another point too that bears on this matter. Defence expenditure is always politically vulnerable in times of peace, so that if procurement programmes are to be maintained it is essential that they be seen to yield direct and tangible benefits – in terms of employment, research and the increased ability to compete – to domestic suppliers. The smaller the proportion of its defence spending a country provides from its own sources, the smaller its total defence spending is likely to be.

In this sphere politics and economics point in the same direction. If public opinion in Europe feels that the organization of Europe's defence is largely in American hands and primarily in the American interest, it will be impossible to generate sufficient support to maintain the equipment, numbers and preparedness of the armed forces of European countries at appropriate levels in terms of either NATO's needs or their own economic potential. This in turn will serve to reinforce the doubts felt in some quarters in the United States as to whether it is worth devoting so much effort to Europe's defence. By contrast the more Europeans feel that the Western Alliance is directed towards their own interests, and that they as well as the Americans are determining its policies and actions, the less difficult will it be to secure the popular support necessary to maintain the armed forces and defence spending of the European allies at levels that will help to ensure the continued large-scale involvement of the United States.

None the less, no one involved in the complex and competitive world of defence procurement would underestimate the problems in bringing about more co-operation in Europe. The complications are immense. The armed forces of the various countries each come forward with their own particular specification for what they need, and the national industries compete vigorously for the largest and most promising shares in the work to be done. Differing views may also have to be reconciled on the appropriate balance between the operational requirements in Europe and the export potential of whatever aeroplane, tank, ship or other piece of equipment is envisaged. Invariably too there is rivalry in both national and corporate terms over the allocation of shareholdings, voting rights and leadership in the company that will be responsible for the enterprise. These were among the issues that caused such difficulty in 1984 and 1985 over the proposed European Fighter Aircraft, and they are likely to recur whenever a major project is under consideration.

They do not, as some would suggest, demonstrate the impossibility of co-operation, but they do show the problems involved in bringing it to fruition. To contemplate them, on the one hand, while considering the impossibility of individual European countries continuing to go it alone, on the other, is to be reminded of Winston Churchill's description of democracy as 'the worst form of government except all those other forms that have been tried from time to time'.[10] Co-operation simply has to be made to work. In due course it will also have to be carried a further stage forward with the countries of Europe agreeing to specialize on particular tasks and areas of expertise, as is already happening in practice, and thereby institutionalizing their dependence on each other.

It is against this background that the view has gained ground in recent years that Europe needs a suitable public forum within the context of the North Atlantic Alliance within which Foreign and Defence Ministers can discuss, and be seen to discuss, every aspect of defence and security. Problems within and outside NATO's geographical limits should be covered as well as how to respond to American initiatives and arms procurement. A number of specific European bodies already operate in the alliance framework, such as the Independent European Programme Group and the Eurogroup, but in their present form they either are too specific in their purpose or lack the right membership. Ideally all Community member states and the non-Community members of NATO as well would participate, but it is hard to see how such an arrangement could be brought about in present circumstances. It is this which makes the rehabilitation of the Western European Union such an attractive option, at least as a first step towards a more comprehensive grouping.

The context of the alliance is the only possible one. The sheer cost that would be involved for Europe in seeking to replace the American nuclear umbrella would be staggering, whether the effort was confined to conventional forces or extended to enhancing the capacity of the British and French nuclear deterrents as well. Even if the European taxpayer was prepared to bear it, which is highly doubtful, many years would elapse before anything as effective as the present arrangements could be put in place, and in all probability they never would be. As President Mitterrand has said: 'The Atlantic Alliance is a reality. It is so unlikely that Europe will be able to assure its own defence in the foreseeable future that I do not think it would be wise to waste time discussing it.'[11]

There is another factor to be borne in mind in these matters that is rarely openly discussed. It is the position of the Federal Republic as the most powerful economy and conventional military power in Western Europe. For as long as the North Atlantic

Alliance continues to exist in more or less its present form that fact can be accommodated within its overall structure. But if the Americans were ever substantially to reduce their European commitment, the Federal Republic's enormous weight in whatever successor arrangement was established would inevitably be highly visible to other Europeans, German public opinion, the Soviet Union and Eastern Europe alike. It is hard to think of a development that would be more unwelcome or disquieting to each of those parties. Latent anti-Germanism in the rest of Europe, Germans' own nightmares about their past and Russian and Eastern European fears of German military might would all be resurrected with consequences that are impossible to foresee. It is not just the military balance between East and West that demands the continuation of the American commitment to the defence of Western Europe. Europe's history in the broadest sense and the legacy it has bestowed require it as well.

The most visible and painful manifestation of that legacy is the division of Europe between a free West and an unfree East with the frontier running through Germany and the balance of power and terror maintained by the superpowers. That division ought to provide a powerful additional incentive for those in the West to strive for the creation of new forms of unity within which liberal and democratic values can flourish and different people live and co-operate freely together. Such unity is needed not just for its own sake, but also to provide a constant reminder to the people of Eastern Europe that there is a better way than the one they are obliged to follow. The more successful the application of the ideas on which the Community is based, the more they will be able to inspire by their example those who are cut off from it.

Western Europeans should never forget the artificiality of the division, nor their responsibility for trying to increase their contacts with the people of the East in such a way as to assist them in leading their own lives and taking their own decisions. For as far ahead as the eye can see, and quite possibly for a long time beyond that, the division will remain. But as and when the scope for Eastern Europeans to widen their links with the West increases, so the Community as such and the member states that constitute it must be ready to respond.

As this book seeks to demonstrate, the overcoming of historic rivalries and the evolution of the Community and other forms of European co-operation are a long, hard process requiring continuous effort over a range of what are often highly technical subjects. It is like building a great cathedral. The vision may be grand and soaring, but it can be translated into reality only through the application of infinite patience, attention to detail and understanding of the particular gifts that each participant brings to bear in the common enterprise. It is difficult to sustain enthusiasm in such circumstances, and easy to lose sight of the importance of what is being attempted.

Symbols

That is why symbols, gestures and rhetoric are so important, but also why, while raising men's and women's eyes, they should not lose touch with reality nor lead to the setting of impossible goals. In addition they should, whenever possible, contribute directly to reinforcing practical forms of unity as well as touching the imagination. Several ideas along these lines have already been proposed, but more is required both to remind the people of Europe of what they have in common and to encourage them to build on it.

In the latter years of the nineteenth century Theodor Herzl, the Viennese writer and journalist who became the principal creator of modern Zionism, wrote in his diary that 'the politics of a whole people – particularly if it is scattered all over the world – can only be made with imponderables that hover high in the air'.[12] What is true of a single people scattered over the world applies with equal force to a number of different peoples sharing the same overcrowded part of it. An element of symbolism, like rhetoric, is essential to any great political enterprise. When something without historical precedent is being attempted it needs to be backed up by symbols that are associated with familiar and well-established political entities. To some, notably those sceptical about the idea or hostile to it, they may seem pretentious and worthy of ridicule. Another problem arises from the way in which symbols, and the importance attached to them, vary from one country to another. It is, therefore, no easy matter to find ones that have the same impact everywhere.

Few are capable of generating more emotion than a flag. More than anything else it signifies a collective pride and sense of identity among those who fly it. For a long time the Community did not have one, and the Council of Europe's circle of gold stars on a blue background was flown unofficially by those wishing to make a European gesture. Eventually a Community emblem in the form of a gold epsilon on a dark blue background was adopted to which, it has since been proposed, a circle of twelve stars should be added. It was hoisted at the World Economic Summit at Williamsburg in the United States in 1983 alongside those of the participating states, including Britain, France, Germany and Italy, to mark the presence of the Commission representing the Community as a whole. The following year it was again raised in London when the summiteers gathered there. It should similarly be flown whenever possible in the member states in order both to assert the existence of the Community and its significance to the country concerned, and to demonstrate that the Community complements the nation state rather than rivalling it.

A European passport falls into a similar category. Any attempt to impose an identical one throughout Europe that took no account of national distinctions would arouse hostility and resentment, and so disunite the peoples concerned rather than promote unity. But the issue of a passport that is both national because it bears distinguishing national features and European because it carries the Community's name as well as the country's is another matter. So long as its possession provides tangible benefits in terms of speeding progress through frontiers it could make the same point as flying the Community and national flags side by side. It would demonstrate that the peoples of the member states, while being separate and distinct, are also bound together and enjoy privileges and rights in each other's countries. Special stamps for intra-Community postage bearing a design common to all the issuing countries coupled with such distinguishing national marks as the Queen's head and the symbol of the French Republic would make the same point.

There are a host of other actions that would help as well, such as the twinning of towns, youth exchange schemes, links between university courses in different countries and cultural festivals. All over Europe private citizens and semi-official bodies are already doing a great deal along these lines. Sometimes the activity is purely social, on other occasions it has a more practical content. Either way it will take a long time to influence deeply rooted national attitudes. But if Europe is to take its place alongside the nation state in the hearts and minds of men and women everywhere, action at a variety of different levels is needed. Those of the heads of state and government, the establishment of common policies and co-operative ventures and the integration of national economies must be backed up by a network of personal relations involving private citizens.

Into the Unknown

Which brings us to the final question to be tackled in this book: what is it all for, and where is it supposed to lead? George Eliot has warned that, 'Among all forms of mistake, prophecy is the most gratuitous',[13] and she was right. If one looks back over any single century in the life-span of the individual member states one cannot but be struck by the extent of the changes that occurred. Few would have predicted them; sometimes they came all in a rush after a long period of stability, and the participants in great events by no means always appreciated the momentous nature of what they were involved in. Sometimes too events turned out to be significant for quite different reasons than those that were intended.

Perhaps the outstanding example of that is Christopher Columbus's voyage in search of India. What a triumph it would have been if he had opened up a westerly route, and how momentous the undertaking must have seemed to him for that reason when he set out. It failed to achieve its objective, but because it led over time and in unpredictable stages to the opening up and development of the American continents it is regarded as one of the turning points of modern history.

Those engaged in European affairs should draw heart from that example. When the Community was launched it was widely seen as a first step towards the fulfilment of the federalist dream of a United States of Europe, and many of those most active in its early days were inspired by that ideal. Now, though one can never be certain about the future, it looks as unlikely to be realized as that of Columbus once he had landed in the New World. Yet something very important and more hopeful for the future than anything else attempted in this part of the world for a long time has been achieved. The old nation states of Europe, and some of the younger ones as well, have found ways to live, work and co-operate together in a single political system – imperfect and incomplete, but a political system none the less. They have also found means of retaining their national identities and pride, while, to a degree that would have seemed impossible forty years ago, draining them of the xenophobia from which stemmed so many wars. At any previous period in European history this would have seemed a Utopian dream.

The idea of a United States of Europe remains as much of a chimera as ever. But the idea of the states of Europe united in a common purpose is now within reach of attainment in some fields at least. Of course it will always be possible to mock both the aim and the progress being made towards it. As has already been pointed out, it is in the nature of a political system that the component parts should forever be engaged in debate and disputation. It is the way in which agreements and common policies are forged in one subject area while the continual search for compromise continues in others.

Progress can be marked in two ways. One is by looking back over one's shoulder from time to time to measure the distance that has been travelled, as for instance by comparing the isolation of the Dutch during their oil shortage crisis in 1973 with the rallying round the British during theirs in 1982. The other is by marking the way in which, despite repeated set-backs and failures, the effort is continuously renewed to achieve certain specific objectives. The completion of the common internal market is one, economic and monetary union is another and the ever closer co-ordination of foreign policies is a third. The way the Community advances has already been likened to the Dance of Echternach: two steps back for every three forward. What is so striking is that notwithstanding such frequent disappointments those engaged on these and other tasks always seek to relaunch their ideas and to move forward again. If the Community ever acquires a motto to accompany its flag the word 'Perseverance' would be a suitable one.

Those who participate in this enterprise can all agree on the objectives of reconciliation, the prevention of war on European soil and the maintenance of representative democracy. They can agree too, as the Treaty of Rome enjoins, that they should try 'to lay the foundations of an ever closer union among the peoples of Europe'. Beyond that there are bound to be differences about ultimate purpose arising out of history, political approach and personality. There are equally bound to be differences in the way those objectives are expressed reflecting different habits of thought and rhetorical traditions.

My own view is that the greatest degree of unity will be achieved if it is based on the continued existence of the nation state rather than on attempts to supplant it. The nation state and the European Union should be seen as enhancing each other, with the latter dependent on the former, extending its scope for effective action and preventing the rivalries inherent in it from running out of control. The union should be achieved, as the Schuman Declaration puts it, through concrete achievements that create a *de facto* solidarity between the countries and peoples concerned. As these are built up so the union itself will take shape and the eyes of its people will be opened to new possibilities.

At this stage it is impossible to forecast what they will be and in any case we have no right to prejudge the future. The task of the present generation should be to find the most effective ways in which the states and people of Europe can live and work together so that subsequent ones may decide for themselves how their union should evolve. As the Community itself is without precedent, so the forms it will adopt are likely to be so as well.

Sources and References

INTRODUCTION

1. J. H. Huizinga, *Mr Europe: A Political Biography of Paul Henri Spaak* (London: Weidenfeld & Nicolson, 1961).
2. Ibid.

I : RHETORIC AND REALITY

1. *The Title*, Act 2.
2. *La Libre Belgique*, 18 October 1984.
3. 'Deux Européens sur Trois: Une Ambition pour l'Europe'. Speech by Valéry Giscard d'Estaing, Brussels, 23 May 1984.
4. Speech to the European Parliament, 29 May 1984.
5. Abba Eban, *The New Diplomacy* (London: Weidenfeld & Nicolson, 1983).
6. *Community Report*, Vol. 4, No. 3, April 1984.
7. Ibid.
8. Richard Mayne, *Postwar* (London: Thames & Hudson, 1983).
9. John Maynard Keynes, *The Economic Consequences of the Peace* (London: Macmillan, 1919).
10. Abba Eban, *The New Diplomacy*, op. cit.
11. Jean Monnet, *Memoirs* (London: Collins, 1978).
12. Ibid.
13. Dean Acheson, *Present at the Creation* (London: Hamish Hamilton, 1970).

14. Jean Monnet, *Memoirs*, op. cit.
15. Ibid.
16. Ibid.
17. *European Unity: A Statement by the National Executive of the Labour Party*, June 1950.
18. Ben Pimlott, *Hugh Dalton* (London: Jonathan Cape, 1985).
19. *The Times*, 3 January 1983.
20. Figures from the European Commission, quoted in the *Financial Times*, 10 May 1985.
21. For a detailed account of their history and operations, see Daniel Strasser, *The Finances of Europe* (Brussels: Commission of the European Communities, 1981).
22. *Working for Europe: The European Commission January 1981 to January 1985* (Brussels: Commission of the European Communities, December 1984).
23. For a detailed and perceptive account of the events surrounding its establishment, see Peter Ludlow, *The Making of the European Monetary System* (London: Butterworths, 1982).
24. Raymond Barre, 'National versus International Solutions for Unemployment', in Andrew Pierre (ed.), *Unemployment and Growth in the Western Economies* (New York: Council on Foreign Relations, 1984).
25. *The World Today*, May 1985.

2 : THE REASONS FOR REALITY

1. Charles de Gaulle, *Memoirs of Hope* (London: Weidenfeld & Nicolson, 1971).
2. Jean Monnet, *Memoirs* (London: Collins, 1978).
3. For an interesting account of these and other relevant matters, see Richard Mayne, *Postwar* (London: Thames & Hudson, 1983).
4. Speech to the Centre of European Policy Studies, 19 November 1984.
5. James Thomas Flexner, *George Washington: The Indispensable Man* (London: Collins, 1976).
6. François Mitterrand, *The Wheat and the Chaff* (London: Weidenfeld & Nicolson, 1982).
7. Charles de Gaulle, *Memoirs of Hope*, op. cit.

8. For a good and concise account of the early years of the Community, the institutional balance, the consequences of de Gaulle's veto and other related matters, see Riccardo Perrissich, 'The Communities' Institutions: Twenty-five Years Later', *Queste Instituzioni*, No. 55, 2nd semester 1982, published by the Olivetti Foundation.

9. See the final communiqué, SEC(72) 3900/E, issued by the Commission of the European Communities, 25 October 1972.

10. Ibid.

11. *Official Journal of the European Communities*, 'Debates of the European Parliament, 1984–85 Session', report of proceedings from 10 to 14 December 1984.

12. Janet Flanner (Genêt), *Paris Journal 1944–1965* (London: Gollancz, 1966).

13. Gordon Craig, *The Germans* (New York: G. P. Putnam's Sons, 1982).

14. Charles de Gaulle, *Memoirs of Hope*, op. cit.

15. *Financial Times*, 21 May 1985.

16. *Die Zeit*, 11 May 1984.

17. *The Times*, 6 May 1985.

18. *Europe* (Agence international d'information pour la presse), 2 February 1985.

19. Luigi Barzini, *The Impossible Europeans* (London: Weidenfeld & Nicolson, 1983); republished under the title *The Europeans* (Harmondsworth: Penguin, 1984).

20. *Die Zeit*, 11 May 1984.

21. Luigi Barzini, *The Impossible Europeans*, op. cit.

22. *Financial Times*, 2 April 1985.

23. Dr Aidan O'Boyle, in the *Irish Press*, 27 November 1984.

24. *Le Figaro*, 16 May 1984.

25. *Financial Times*, 30 March 1985.

26. Commission document COM(79) 462, *Reference Paper on Budgetary Questions*, 12 September 1979.

27. John Newhouse, 'The Diplomatic Round', *New Yorker*, 22 October 1984.

3 : TOWARDS A BETTER WAY

1. Speech to the European Parliament, 16 February 1984.

2. *The Bulletin*, 24 September 1984.

3. David Dilkes (ed.), *The Diaries of Sir Alexander Cadogan, 1938–1945* (London: Cassell, 1971), Introduction 1884–1938.
4. *Le Monde*, 3 October 1984.
5. *Le Quotidien*, 3 October 1984.
6. 'Deux Européens sur Trois: Une Ambition pour l'Europe'. Speech by Valéry Giscard d'Estaing, Brussels, 23 May 1984.
7. Jean Monnet, *Memoirs* (London: Collins, 1978).

4 : JOURNEY TO AN UNKNOWN DESTINATION

1. Janet Flanner (Genêt), *Paris Journal 1944–1965*, op. cit.
2. Quoted by Chancellor Kohl in a speech to the Bundestag, 4 May 1983.
3. Speech opening the proceedings for the renewal of the ACP–EEC Convention, Luxembourg, 6 October 1983.
4. Quoted in Erich Guner, *The Political System of Switzerland* from *Modern Switzerland* (Palo Alto: Society for the Promotion of Science and Scholarship, Inc., 1978), pp. 339–59.
5. *Financial Times*, 24 May 1984.
6. Speech by Malcolm Rifkind and delivered on his behalf by Baroness Young to the Maison de l'Europe Franco-British Day, Paris, 31 January 1985.
7. *Financial Times*, 30 May 1985.
8. Raymond Barre, 'National versus International Solutions for Unemployment', in Andrew Pierre (ed.), *Unemployment and Growth in the Western Economies* (New York: Council on Foreign Relations, 1984).
9. Douglas Hurd, 'Political Co-operation', *International Affairs*, Summer 1981.
10. Speech to the House of Commons, 11 November 1947.
11. *The Times*, 24 October 1984.
12. Carl E. Schorske, *Fin-de-Siècle Vienna* (New York: Alfred A. Knopf, 1980).
13. *The Mill on the Floss*, 1860.

Select Bibliography

Acheson, Dean, *Present at the Creation* (London: Hamish Hamilton, 1970)

Barzini, Luigi, *The Impossible Europeans* (London: Weidenfeld & Nicolson, 1983); republished under the title *The Europeans* (Harmondsworth: Penguin, 1984)

Craig, Gordon, *The Germans* (New York: G. P. Putnam's Sons, 1982)

De Gaulle, Charles, *Memoirs of Hope* (London: Weidenfeld & Nicolson, 1971)

Deniau, Jean François, *L'Europe Interdite* (Paris: Editions du Seuil, 1977)

Eban, Abba, *The New Diplomacy* (London: Weidenfeld & Nicolson, 1983)

Flanner, Janet (Genêt), *Paris Journal 1944–1965* (London: Gollancz, 1966)

Huizinga, J. H., *Mr Europe: A Political Biography of Paul Henri Spaak* (London: Weidenfeld & Nicolson, 1961)

Keynes, John Maynard, *The Economic Consequences of the Peace* (London: Macmillan, 1919)

Ludlow, Peter, *The Making of the European Monetary System* (London: Butterworths, 1982)

Mayne, Richard, *Postwar* (London: Thames & Hudson, 1983)

Monnet, Jean, *Memoirs* (London: Collins, 1978)

Noel, Emile, *The European Community: How It Works* (Brussels: Commission of the European Communities, 1979)

SELECT BIBLIOGRAPHY

Shonfield, Andrew, *Europe: Journey to an Unknown Destination* (Harmondsworth: Penguin, 1973); an expanded version of the BBC Reith Lectures, 1972

Strasser, Daniel, *The Finances of Europe* (Brussels: Commission of the European Communities, 1981)

Index